ALBANIAN HISTORICAL FOLKSONGS
1716 - 1943

*A Survey of Oral Epic
Poetry from Southern
Albania with Original Texts
Collected and Translated
by*

P. J. RUCHES

ARGONAUT INC., PUBLISHERS
CHICAGO   MCMLXVII

LIBRARY OF CONGRESS CATALOGUE CARD NO. 67-29121

TABLE OF CONTENTS

TO
THE SINGERS OF THE SONGS

By the rivers of Babylon, there we sat down,
yea, we wept when we remembered Zion.

PREFACE

A people's collective memory of persons and events, crystalized in the verse of its anonymous bards, is a primary source of historical data. Orally transmitted from generation to generation—each adding its own contribution to the whole—it remains intact to the extent that it is still pertinent to its cultural matrix. It is lost only when the latter undergoes a radical transformation.

Two contrasting examples, suffice. On one hand, there are no illiterate French farmers who can recite by rote fragments of the *Chanson de Roland*. This is because sweeping changes destroyed the social context in which the mediaeval epic was conceived. Conversely, the Byzantine cycle relating the deeds of the border warrior Digenes Acritas in battling the Saracens in Asia Minor—roughly contemporary with the period of the *chanson*—survives. It lives in hours-long episodes on the lips of Pontian and Cypriote Greek peasants. In this instance, even unconsciously, this folk has every reason to consider the present in historical continuity with struggles that took place centuries ago.[1]

Professional ethnologists and historians are due an apology, since the present work by one who is neither, trespasses on both their fields. It is, however, possible for one who has not been inducted formally into either of these academic disciplines to reason historically and appreciate as well the accumulated force of oral tradition. There is even hope that a meaningful synthesis may emerge, although a critical evaluation of it may be beyond this writer's scope.

The present volume is the outcome of an intensive, self-imposed study involved in sifting the background of the long-standing Greco-Albanian border dispute. During the course of that study, from which an earlier work emerged[2], much of the material utilized in the present one was examined. Its use then would have expanded that volume unnecessarily.

---

[1] See Henri, Gregoire, *Digenes Acritas,* New York, 1948, in Greek. Subsequent works in Greek cited below will be indicated by an asterisk (*). See also bibliography.

[2] *Albania's Captives,* Chicago, 1965, subsequently referred to as *AC.*

That this material may be regarded as supplementary for the reader with a specialized interest is indicated by the numerous citations to the earlier work made herein. It also may absolve this writer from lengthy but sometimes necessary recapitulation.

The seventy four ballads—texts and translations—forming the core of the present work are, perhaps, the first integral corpus of historical folksongs from what is now southern Albania to appear in English. They cover a period of 227 years.

Versions of many of them have appeared in Albanian collections made over a half-century ago. A compilation of these collections, many of them long out of print, has been made in modern transcription and published by the Folklore Institute of Tirana.[3]

Another priceless source are the works, gratefully acknowledged, of Alexander Ch. Mammopoulos, a native of an Albanian-speaking Greek village in the region of Argyrocastron who has devoted a lifetime to Epirote folklore studies. He is presently resident in Athens and his works, published in Greek, have been consulted constantly by the author.

Ultimately, however, the primary source of any published version is the people themselves. This source has been used extensively and without acknowledgement owing to the reluctance of the otherwise most helpful informants. Many are simple men and women of the people with relatives in Communist Albania and thus understandably concerned lest such acknowledgement prove harmful to their kin. Some of these informants are themselves refugees from Enver Hoxha's Chinese night soil factory. Others are residents and citizens either of Greece or of the United States for many years prior to the establishment of the "People's Republic." All of them learned to chant these songs as part of the lore learned at their mothers' breasts. While unacknowledged singly, they are due the lion's share of the collective credit. Without them, this book could not have been.

The living folk itself holds the key to the relationship between these songs and the cultural history that gave them shape. Even when the oral material diverges from historic exactitude (and it does so rarely), it remains true to the sentiments and understanding of its possessors. Were a historian to ignore it entirely—and it is difficult to do so in dealing with a region whose speech possessed no written form until recently—he would often have recourse to an uncertain intuition.[4] Diplo-

---

[3] Institut i Folklorit, *Mbledhës të Hershëm të Folklorit Shqiptar, 1635-1912* (3 vols.), Tirana, 1962. With footnotes of "Marxist" commentary by the compilers.

[4] While there was no real written *speech*, there was a written language—Greek. In addition, there was a tiny output of books in Albanian utilizing a modified Greek alphabet, one of the earliest being the diglott (colloquial Greek and Albanian) New

mats, politicians, scholars and journalists have ample means of making themselves heard. But shepherds and peasants, merchants and warriors have not been silent either. They, too, deserve to be heard. Whatever else this volume may accomplish, it will certainly do this.

A dispassionate stance would serve the victims of tyranny ill indeed, and this author will not try to practice apathy where the dignity of man has been violated and self-determination of peoples has been denied. But passion does not preclude a scrupulous regard for the facts. This would go without saying were there not those for whom the facts are unwelcome and who may be expected to react accordingly.

At the same time, the truth would be ill served if the view taken of the same event in the ballads of the two diametrically opposed communities were disregarded. The Christian and Moslem ballads read together shed much light on the feelings within each community generated by the events themselves. In two ballads only (Nos. 23 and 53), we step outside the two communities of Albania's present southern prefectures to weigh the attitude of their northern neighbors, the Ghegs.

The Albanians living north of the Genoussas or Shkumbi River— i.e. the Ghegs—have only tangentally concerned themselves with the places and events of the south. As different in speech from the people of Northern Epirus as the Serbs are from the Bulgars and as divergent in social organization as the Berbers are from the peoples of southern Europe, the two have little in common. With the Moslems of Epirus, the Ghegs have, true, a common religious tie. But this is no more than the tie with other Balkan converts to Islam. With the Orthodox Christian majority of Epirus, the Ghegs (save, perhaps, the miniscule Orthodox group in the region of Elbasan closest to the Shkumbi) have had few ties at all.[5]

Testament of Gregory the Argyrocastran, bishop of Euboia, printed in 1827 in Corfu. Bishop Gregory (Mexis) at the time was a fugitive from imprisonment by the Turko-Albanians in Euboia where he had been accused of masterminding the Greek uprising there. One of the last products of this literature was Constantine Christophorides' (Kristoforidhi) *Lexicon of the Albanian Language,* Athens, 1904. Kristoforidhi was not an Epirote, but an Albanian from Elbasan. A successful parallel to this usage of Greek letters is the literature in Turkish produced by the Cappadocian Greeks. This included the Bible, religious works and two newspapers in Constantinople: *Anatole-Anadolu* and *Asia.* This type of literature was no more Turkish—or Albanian—than Yiddish is German.

[5] It is quite different with the Greeks of Thessaly, Aetolo-Acarnania, Macedonia and the Peloponnese whose folksongs tell the same events and express the same sentiments as those of the "Christian Albanians" of Northern Epirus. To compare them textually would make a volume twice the size of the present work. The author has, however, indicated wherever possible, where such Greek ballads have been published for those who may wish to do so.

An exception was the common participation in the fifteenth century Christian uprising associated with the name of Skanderbeg. This, however, was a *Christian* rising involving others besides the Albanians. Considering the context of its time, in addition to its heterogeneous nature, it can hardly be called a *national* upsurge. The Gheg Albanian conversion to Islam, indeed, took place as a result of its failure. The failure, however, did not affect the religion of those further south who chose the conqueror's faith somewhat later and under different social and political pressures. It did not affect Greeks and Serbs who had fought in the same ranks, except to steel their determination to rise again. Finally, it did not touch the Albanian-speaking Epirote *stradioti* whose descendents are still to be found in Italy. The modern Albanian nationalist myth, eagerly promulgated to prove a national cohesion historically non-existant, is another story.

The present Albanian government is an interesting illustration of a four-way split. The north-south dichotomy is mirrored in the fact that the ruling Bolshevik clique's members are nearly all from the south. The religious split is displayed by the fact that, although top level posts are evenly distributed between Christians and Moslems, the Moslems monopolize nearly all the key power posts. The first split is geographic, but what underlies the second is social and it is the rarely alluded to premise behind the entire Ottoman and post-Ottoman history of Albania south of the Shkumbi.

Lest those who read the foregoing attribute to the author a general anti-Islamic animus, it must be stated here expressly and sincerely that such an attitude is disavowed. It could be maintained only by someone blind or insensitive to the positive aspects of Moslem civilization and ignorance of its best representatives.

The Ottoman state and its military-feudal caste—an offspring of which is modern Albania—were, however, only rarely repositories of these values. The Moslem conquerors did not behave as they did because they believed in the Unity rather than in the Trinity of the Godhead, but because they were conquerors. The Moslems of Epirus did not bow to the God of Islam for love of Him, but because their material advantage was to identify themselves with that conqueror's naked force. In turn, the conqueror allowed them to become his proxies in the exercise of that force to subjugate, humiliate and expropriate all those who would not do likewise.

That empire died, but its mentality lived on in Albania as more than a vestige for another half century. The story is recapitulated with Albania's continued practice of unadulterated Stalinism. Today, Stalin is a rotting corpse interred within the Kremlin's shadow. His paranoid system of misery lives on in Albania. A current Soviet poet observes:

> It seems to me there is a telephone
>   installed in his coffin
> And he is still sending instructions
>   to Enver Hoxha.
> NO—Stalin has not thrown in his ticket;
>   death, he believes, can be rectified.
> We carried him away—
>   threw him out of the mausoleum,
> But how shall we remove Stalin
>   from within Stalin's heirs?[6]

The parallel here between what the Ottoman Empire and Stalin's Soviet one represented for Albania is in the worship by both of brute force. To understand the latter's impact on Albania's rulers, it would not be amiss to review the former's.

Most of the events that split the northern portion of the Greek seaboard province of Epirus as well as part of Macedonia into Moslem and Christian communities transpired in the sixteenth and seventeenth centuries. Although this process was by no means complete, the full force of this wave had been spent as the eighteenth century dawned.

It is then that our narrative begins.

PYRRHUS J. RUCHES

New York, 1967

[6] Yevgeny Yevtushenko, *Stalin's Heirs*.

AN ERA BEGINS
(1716)

In the eighteenth century, Europe no longer trembled before the "Terrible Turke." Nevertheless, as the century opened, the Ottoman Empire was still believed to be a force to be reckoned with. It was not long, however, before the first signs of its prolonged death throes began to become apparent to astute observers. The Sublime Porte's war with Venice, resulting in the Turkish reconquest of the Peloponnese after a campaign of only 101 days, was the last major triumph of Ottoman arms in Europe. Emboldened by this easy sweep, an Ottoman army under Kara Mustafa Pasha and a fleet under Djanum Hodja invaded Corfu the next year— 1716.[7].

With the brutal Ottoman resubjugation of the Peloponnese fresh before their eyes, the Christians of Epirus watched the siege of Corfu with great anxiety. With the fall of the Peloponnese, Venice's Greek septinsular possessions had become the one nearby haven to which they could flee from persecution, for it had never been under the Sultan's rule. The Moslems of Epirus, too, watched the siege with anxiety, for many of their sons, having returned with booty from the sack of the Peloponnese, now landed on the beach of Corfu and commenced the siege of the castle. These besiegers included Muhtar Bey of Tepeleni, son of the formidable bandit Meco Hyso and grandfather of Ali Pasha of Yannina.[8] Many years later, in the *Alipasiad,* composed in Greek at the tyrant's behest by his official balladeer, Haxhi Shekreti, it is recalled of Muhtar that "he, too, became a *sayid*[9] and passed away with honor."

The Ottoman failure to take the fortress of Corfu, coupled with the final expulsion of the Turks from Hungary that year and the next, was the *coup de grace* in Western Europe to the myth of Ottoman invinci-

---

[7] Immanuel Bekkerus, (ed.), *Historia Politica et Patriarchica Constantinopoleos Epirotica, de rebus Epiri,* Frag. V, pp. 255-256.

[8] Spyridon P. Aravantinos, **History of Ali Pasha Tepelenli,* Athens, 1895, p. 3.

[9] *sayid* (Arabic): a Moslem slain in battle against infidels.

bility, although a full two centuries were to elapse before the Balkan Christians were able to extricate themselves fully from its grasp.[10]

In the siege of Corfu, there was a direct armed confrontation between the Christians and Moslems of Epirus, for there were many fugitive Epirotes among the defenders of Corfu. And there is little doubt where Christian sympathies throughout Epirus lay. The Christian Epirotes of what is now "southern Albania" have chosen to remember not the Albanian bandit, Meco Hyso's son, but the heroic defenders of Corfu, with their prayers.

The reference in this song to St. Spyridon, Patron of Corfu "who went to sea and came to land," recalls how the remains of the early bishop of Trimythus, Cyprus, came to rest in their present shrine. A priest named George Kalochaeretes, who saved them from the sack of the Church of the Holy Apostles in Constantinople's fall, brought them first to Parga in Epirus and thence to Corfu aboard ship in 1456.

St. Demetrius' (Dimitris') Day is Oct. 26.

1.

Dolla ditën e Shënmitrit	I went on St. Dimitris' Day
në divan të Stambollitit;	To Stambolitis' sitting room;
Pashë zonjat e Moresë	Grecian ladies I beheld
të bardha si cip' e vesë.	White as an eggshell.
Ca këndonin, ca vajtonin	Some sang, others wept
për ca trima që lëftonin:	For some braves in battle:
"Biri, o, trima tanë	Oh sons, our warriors
lëftonin Korfuz kalanë	Fought in Corfu's Castle
se Korfuzi ka të zonë,	Because Corfu has a master,
të Zonë Shën Spiridhonë.	Master Saint Spyridon.
"Spiridhon-o, shënjt i gjallë,	Oh, Spyridon, living saint,
re ndë det e dolle mb'anë,	Who went to sea and came to land,
shpëtoje Korfuz Kalanë!	Save the Castle of Corfu!
O, Spiridhoni Spilesë,	Oh, Spyridon of the Cave,
thërri Turqit për besë	For the faith cut down the Turks
një sahat njëqint e pesë!	One hundred and five in an hour!
"Tetë kandile t'argjënda,	Eight silver candles,
katër jashtë e katër mbrënda,	Four outside and four within,
tri të lara me flori,	Three plated with gold,
as e fal, o, Perëndi!	Be thanks to Thee, oh God!

[10] The Ottoman garrison at Temesvar surrendered to Prince Eugene of Savoy on Nov. 25, 1716. Hungary was relinquished formally by Turkey in the Treaty of Passarovitz on July 21, 1718.

ARMATOLES AND KLEPHTS
(1750-1800)

There were two outstanding and closely related factors in the continual state of unrest in Ottoman-occupied Greece throughout the eighteenth century. One was the unflagging—and often undeserved—optimism of the populace that outside aid would help to oust the Ottoman Empire from the Balkans and curb the oppressive power of its local Moslem collaborators. The other was the peculiar institution of the "armatolik" which continually proved a double-edged weapon for the Porte. The *armatoloi* were Christian bands headed by a "captain" whose function it was to assist the Turkish authorities in the suppression of brigandage and rebellion. Unfortunately for the Ottomans, the *armatoloi* were also a ready-made guerrilla force ready to turn their weapons and deadly skill in mountain fighting upon their masters. And this is what many *armatoloi* did repeatedly at every clash between Turkey and a European power. Thus the *armatoloi* became synonymous with *klephtai,* brigands—a name the authorities gave them in exasperation, but which they carried with pride.[11]

A whole body of modern Greek literature—both oral and written—is a celebration of the lives and heroic deaths of individual *klephtai* who, certainly far from all blamelessness, nevertheless were regarded much as the English Saxons regarded the Robin Hoods who resisted England's Norman conquerors. The one insurance that the Porte had against these disturbers of the "pax othomanica" was the privileged Moslem minority of natives "turned Turk." These, "by adopting the faith of their conquerors . . . were allowed to retain possession of their farms and property. The Christians became serfs, and were set to work on the lands under a system of feudal servitude which was exceedingly onerous."[12]

The Bosnian *dahijas* in Bosnia and Serbia and the Albanian Moslems

[11] Of the many accounts of the *armatoloi* and *klephtai* we cite two, both by participants: General Theodore Kolokotronis, *The Greek War of Independence,* London, 1892 (repr. Chicago, 1967) and General Makriyannis, *Memoirs: 1797-1864.* Edited and translated by H. A. Lidderdale. Oxford 1966.

[12] Leon Dominian, *Frontiers of Language and Nationality in Europe,* The American Geographical Society, N.Y., 1917.

3

in many parts of European Turkey, and especially throughout Greece,
played such a role. In southern Greece, in fortified villages such as
Bardouni near Sparta and mediaeval Mistra, or in administrative centers
such as Tripolitsa, they acted as the Sultan's watchdogs against rebellion.
An Albanian Moslem author admits:

> The Turks found comrades in hard battle and in faith in the
> Albanians, and the Albanians found a master in the Turks who
> opened up a broad and free avenue to them to do whatever their
> heart desired. Albania was governed by Albanians according to their
> customs, and Turkey gave them whatever they wanted—property,
> honor, as much arms as they desired and as much freedom as they
> needed; and Turkey found among them bravery, faith and blood
> spilled without regret.[13]

The Albanians provided the Ottoman Empire with thirty-six grand
viziers, including the illustrious line of the Köprülüs, a hundred heads
of the Janissary Corps and countless military and civil functionaries. It
was, in fact, only when the Sultans angered *their* keepers, the Janissaries
in Constantinople, that this element wavered at all in its loyalty, for the
Moslem Albanians' ties with that body included kinship, mutual interest
and a common religious bond in the sect founded by the corps' patron
saint—the dervish order of "Hazret Hunkâr" Hadji Bektash Veli.[14]
The Turks stood less in danger of Christian revolts in the large urban
centers such as Constantinople and Smyrna. The Greeks there were the
leading element of the empire's mercantile class, along with the Armenians
and the Sephardic Jews. Their weapon in defending themselves from
their masters' oppression was the bribe; that of the Greek mountaineer
in the Balkans was the sword. There, in the hills where the *klephtai*
had their *limeria* or hideouts, a savage war without quarter continually

---

[13] Teqi Selenica, *Albania in 1927*, (in Albanian), pp. 8, 9. This phenomenon of
not accommodation, but collaboration, with their conquerors survived Turkish domi-
nation and was in considerable evidence quite recently. See *AC*, pp. 154-55. As
an Albanian proverb puts it: *"Tek është kordha është besa,"* ("Where the sword is,
there is the faith"), a survival of the mediaeval *cuius regio, eius religio.*

[14] J. K. Birge, *The Bektashi Order of Dervishes,* London, 1937. The virtual
identity of the Janissary Corps and the order is also shown clearly by the *gülbenk*
or war cry recited in unison by the officers of the corps after the meal prepared
for them in the palace kitchen. This followed the tri-monthly payment of rations
to the troops. The text is as follows:
"Allah, Allah! There is no God save He alone. With bared head and pure
breast, let my sword take blood! Many heads are cut off here and none asks
why. By God, our might and our sword bring loss to the enemy; our service
belongs to the Sultan. By threes, sevens, forties, the Moslem war cry, the light
of the Prophet, the generosity of Ali, unto our spiritual teacher and master Hadji
Bektash Veli we shout: 'It is He!' "

flared. The heroes of this resistance live on in songs passed down from generation to generation to our own day.

We know little about the subject and the events of following song, which took place about 1750[15], some decades before the great precursor of the Greek Revolution, the so-called "Orlov uprising" encouraged by Catherine the Great.[16] Captain Bedo is believed to have been a native of the now only partially Christian village of Alarupi near Korytsa who met his death at the hands of an assassin sent by Ahmet Pasha of Ochrida —the Ahmet Pasha of the song. The Souli of the text is, in my opinion, a small and now entirely Moslem village near Viglista, as indicated by the reference to Starovo nearby. It would appear from indications here, however, that the village was still Christian when these events took place. This Souli, of course, should not be confused with the famous Souli of Thesprotia.

2.

More Bedo shapërdani,
ndë Stamboll të vatë nami:
Lëfton Bedo Kapetani!

O Bedo, swift of foot,
To Stamboul your fame has travelled:
Captain Bedo battles!

Bini, o, trima, të lëftojmë!

Strike, oh warriors, let's fight!

Ahmet Pashë binish gjatë,
ku i con ata bajrak?
Sulit t'i prishëm kalatë!

Long-capoted Ahmet Pasha,
Whither do you send the standard?
To Souli to wreck its towers!

Bini, o, trima, të lëftojmë!

Strike, oh warriors, let's fight!

More Gegë gunë gjetë,
as e shihni se më s'mbetë?
Lëfton Bedua e Suli vetë!

Hey you Ghegs in long fleeces,
See you not one of you is left?
Bedo fights and Souli itself!

Bini, o, trima, të lëftojmë!

Strike, oh warriors, let's fight!

Qysh bënet puna jonë?
Përpiqu, Bedo, përpiqu!
Si birbili ndë Prill digju:

How shall our work be done?
Struggle, Bedo, struggle!
Like an April nightingale he sounded:

"Bini, o, trima, të lëftojmë!"

"Strike, oh warriors, let's fight!"

Që Stamboll e tatëpjetë,
nd'atë Starovën e shkretë,
o, Turq të zinjë, më s'mbetë!

From Stamboul to yonder,
To Starovo the barren,
Oh blackened Turks, you tarried not!

Bini, o, trima, të lëftojmë!

Strike, oh warriors, let's fight!

One of the regions that "turned Turk" was that known today as

[15] Cf. Alexander Ch. Mammopoulos, *Epirus: Folklore, Customs, Ethnography,* 2 vols., Vol. II, Athens, p. 23.

[16] Constantine N. Sathas, *Turkish-Occupied Greece, 1453-1821,* Athens, 1869 (stereotype reprint 1962), p. 460 *et seq.*

Kurveleshi or Labëria, the principal center of which is Tepeleni, the former Titoupolis, an important shrine of the Bektashi sect in former European Turkey and the birthplace of Ali Pasha of Yannina, about whom more later. Bordering it on the seacoast, however, are the predominantly Christian villages of the districts of Chimarra and Delvino. Of the villages of Chimarra proper, Chimarra itself, Drymades, and Paliasa are primarily Grecophone, while Vouno, Piliouri, Koudesi and Keparon speak Albanian primarily. Adjoining villages of the district of Delvino, such as Nivitsa Boubari, St. Basil, Loukovo, Pikerni and Senitsa, are sometimes considered as part of Chimarra with which they are linked historically. Under the protection of Venice from 1463 to 1518, they were forced to become a nominal part of the Ottoman Empire upon the Venetian evacuation of that portion of the mainland. Under the terms of capitulation accepted by Turkey's representative, Elaz Bey Vlorë, a converted native of the district, they retained their arms and privileges of self-government.[17]

Because the Chimarriotes were both willing and able to resist encroachments and any diminution of these privileges by their apostate former kin, they provided a constant inspiration to their Epirote countrymen less capable of such dogged resistance. The Porte, in turn, did with them what it did elsewhere in such regions as Mani in the Peloponnese, Souli in Thesprotia and, afield, in the Lebanon. It recognized the *status quo* and left it to local Moslem rulers to whittle away at the privileges of autonomy. When that happened, conflict was inevitable and the Porte had recourse to three possible ways of dealing with it. It could cool off the local Moslems, dispatch a costly force to crush the Christians, or, it could have the more recalcitrant Christian leaders lured to their deaths and then deal more easily with "reasonable elements." All three methods, alternately or concurrently, were used against Chimarra's defenders. It is to such incidents that the following songs refer. Both Ghikas Thanasi and Kyriakos Kapasis were natives of Keparon. Thanasi's family had moved there from Borshi in Kurveleshi where another branch of the family apostasized. He was the nephew of Abdullah Pasha Vasilaj ('Abdyl Vasili') who governed in Syria. Mammopoulos notes[18] that the Moslem branch survived in Ahmet Bey Vasilaj who, in 1944, was living in Santi Quaranta, and his son, Abdyl Vasilaj, who was the postmaster then of Delvino.

The first song tells of how Ghikas Thanasi, on the pretext of an invitation to enlist in a force of *armatoles,* was lured to Yannina where he was drugged and executed. The second is, in actuality, a plaint bemoan-

[17] *AC,* pp. 30-32.

[18] *Op. cit.* Vol. II, pp. 21, 22.

ing the fact that brave Captain Kapasis' sons failed to follow in his footsteps. (The month of St. Andrew is December).

3.

Nëndë muaj i Shënëndre,
Gjikë Thanasi lule,
t'erdhi një joll tesqere.
Janinë u nise vajte
të shkruesh në ilefe.

On the ninth of St. Andrew,
Blossoming Ghikas Thanasi,
A road pass came to you.
To Yannina you sallied forth
To enlist in the troops.

Seç t'a bënë me hile;
të ftuan në kafene,
të helmuan me kafe
e të vun' në batare.

With treachery they did you in;
They bid you to the coffeehouse,
They poisoned you with coffee
And put you before a firing squad.

Plumbi shkoj po ty se pe;
në rrip të pallaskave
të këputi. Re për dhe.
Harrite dy fjalë the:
"O, ç'm'bëtë gruan të ve
edhe mëmën kallogre."

The shot went through, but you saw it not;
On the thong of the cartridge box
It cut you. To the earth you fell.
Just two words could you utter:
"Oh, you've made my wife a widow
And my mother a nun."

Pashanë shtrëmbër e pe:
"Abdyl Vasilit i the:
shtëpinë amanet t'a lë."

Upon the pasha he looked askance:
"Say unto Abdul Vasili:
I leave you my house undefended."

4.

Dielli që lëshon çika,
hane-hane o, Qirjako,
të kërkon Kapetan Gjika
të veç armët e florinjta;
të do për shtiqe të liga,
tek e liga, tek është nderi,
o, Qirjako iliveri!

Like the sun that casts its rays,
Oh handsome Kyriako,
Captain Ghika seeks you
To don your golden armor;
For a stand of strength he needs you,
For a stand of strength, of honor,
Oh Kyriako the star!

O, iliver efanua,
sorkadhi që shkel me thua!

Oh shining star,
Roe that treads on tiptoes!

Që fëmij' u rrefëgua,
hajdut maleve langua,
kaqë vjet nuk u dëgjua.
Më qafë kur u tregua,
gjithë fshati u gëzua!

From a youth he fled,
A klepht in the hills, a hound,
For many years none heard of him.
When he appeared upon the ridge,
The whole village rejoiced!

Kur ngjitesh malit përpjetë,
ti jatak keshe okshetë;
bukënë t'a binin Vlletë.
U mirrnje arhonëve djemtë,
i nisje Lëbozhd përpjetë.

When you climbed upon the hills,
The mountain crags were your bed;
The Vlachs brought you your bread.
The notables' sons you gathered,
You sent them up to Libozdi.

Qirjako, s'të ngjanë djemtë;
hap varrë të dalish vetë
të rrëmbesh pallën e shkretë.
Të keshe Vanthinë djalë
s'të lijë hakën pa marrë.

Kyriako, your children are unlike you;
Open your grave and come out yourself
To seize your barren sword.
Had you Evanthia for a son,
She would not abandon your cause.

One of the weapons used by the Moslems to ensure their superiority and to encourage apostasy was a cruel system of taxation from which Moslems were exempt. A current Albanian textbook elucidates:

> As a means of coercing the inhabitants to embrace Islam, in addition to religious discrimination in social life, the Turks enforced the policy of discrimination in the field of taxation as well. Of these taxes, the chief place was assumed by a tax called *djiza*.
> At the beginning of the sixteenth century, the *djiza* was imposed uniformly from Albania to Roumelia and amounted to 40-50 *aktche* per house. By the beginning of the seventeenth century, however, in Albania and especially in the Sandjak of Valona, it reached 305 *aktche* annually.
> About the middle of the seventeenth century, the campaign of islamization had reached a climax and the *djiza* had been increased to 325 *aktche*.
> Despite this, 10,741 Christian families remained in this sandjak who resisted this annihilating conversion tax.
> The satanical instrument, having been created, proceeded to do its work. The *djiza* was imposed by the inspectors of revenues upon all the Christian villages acording to the aforementioned proportion at 325 to 355 *aktche*. Families embracing Islam were exempt and their proportionate part of the tax was added to the burden of the remainder and reached 780 *aktche*. It is well understood that no other choice remained to the Christians but the mass abandonment of their ancestral religion.[19]

It was the villages of Chimarra and Delvino, again, which took the fullest advantage of a second and much harder choice—they resisted and made good their resistance. They were not capable of understanding that they had no choice—and they would neither pay the tax nor convert. This stubbornness preserved both their faith and their national identification through the nineteenth and early twentieth centuries, culminating in the declaration of Chimarriote Greek independence during the Balkan Wars by Major Spyromelios on November 5, 1912.[20]

5.

Qasi, o, shokë të rimë	Close in, companions, let's sit
as të hame, as të pime,	Neither to eat nor to drink,
po t'u dëftoj istorinë	But that I may show you the story
për sebep të vëndit synë,	For the sake of our country,
për Nivie' e Shën Vasinë.	About Nivitsa and Saint Basil.
"Vate Kost' Aleks Janinë;	"Kostas Alexis, go to Yannina;
foli rëndë me Mudirë."	Speak loudly with the governor."

[19] *History of Albania*, Institute of History and Language, Tirana, 1959, (in Albanian) pp. 366-368.

[20] *AC* p. 65.

Me të dalë nga saraji
i tha dy fjalë Pashaj:
"Mbaj, kapetanë, mbaj,
dhe nga dovleti mos qaj."

At his exit from the palace,
Two words the pasha told him:
"Patience, Captain, patience,
Raise no outcry from the empire."

"Dhe nga dovleti të jetë,
ne s'e japim të tretë;
gjithë kemi për të vdekë."

"Even though it's from the empire,
We'll not pay a third in taxes;
We are all determined to die."

6.

Erdhe Mehmet Beu Delvinë,
hedh një dyfek kërcellimë
për Nivic' e Shën Vasinë,
Senicën e Kakodhiqnë.

Mehmet Bey Delvina came,
He fired a thunderous gun
On Nivitsa and Saint Basil,
Senitsa and Kakodiki.

Në Nivic' e kanë synë:
"Nivicjotë, ç'ini të marë,
pse s'bëni kabull kandarë?"

On Nivitsa they fix their eyes:
"Nivitsans, what has possessed you,
Why will you not pay the tax?"

Këta xhevapin e dhanë:
"Njëqind vjet rrim në hapsanë!"

Such was the reply they gave:
"We'll sit in jail a hundred years!"

A "LION" IS BORN
(1744-1788)

"Merhemetli Vizir Ali Veli Arslan Tepedelenli, Rumeli Valesi, Yanya ve Trikal Pasasu ve Dervedat Nazir."

"His Puissance Vizier Ali Veli the Tepelenian Lion, Vali of Roumelia, Pasha of Yannina and Trikkala and Supervisor General of the Passes."

These were the resounding Ottoman titles borne by the ruler of Epirus and *de facto* king of Greece at the height of his power. Under their breaths, however, the victims of his cruelty called him by other epithets, "Ali the beast" and "son of Hanko the slut" being among the milder.[21] The twentieth Ottoman governor since 1550[22], he was five feet five in height, with blue eyes and a fair complexion. He was inclined to corpulence in his old age when he wore a billowing white beard easily equal to the best in an empire where such adornment was prized. To complete the picture, we need only add the *teslim taç,* the 12-pleated cap of a Bektashi initiate, which he habitually wore. A Greek folksong recalls that "he was meetly praised . . . and inscribed a Janissary,"[23] and, while he never served actively in that infamous corps, both his strength and subsequent downfall were not unrelated to the corps' power and its final destruction. Many strangers afar hailed him as an Ottoman Bonaparte, while those who knew him best despised him as a provincial Caligula. Woe to the subject who was unwilling to deed him a possession he coveted. Such a subject would be tortured to death and the property confiscated. And woe to those upon whom the pasha's paranoid suspicion fell. Because he suspected a married Greek woman with whom he had dallied of being the mistress of his son Muhtar, he had her and seventeen other women—the

---

[21] *AC,* pp. 37-42.

[22] According to John, M.D. Lambrides, *Epirotic Studies: Description of the City of Ioannina,* Vol. 1, Athens, 1887.

[23] " *ἦταν ἄξιος πεναμένος...καὶ γιανίτσαρος γραμμένος.* "

10

others being innocent matrons of impeccable character—drowned in the lake of Yannina.[24]

When Mustafa Pasha Delvina, a longtime foe who had slipped through Ali's fingers once, was finally captured, he was brought as a "guest" to his citadel where he died, the pasha said, a "natural" death—of starvation. Both the historian and the student of psychopathology will find Ali's career not without interest. For a parallel among their rulers, learned Epirotes could recall only the savage mediaeval despot Thomas Preljuboviç, of whom a chronicler wrote: "all depravity is small before the depravity of Thomas."[25]

Between 1638 and 1640, a Turkish dervish from Asia Minor named Hüseyn visited Tepeleni's Bektashi shrine and remained. Who he was, no one knew. He was believed, however, to have been a native of Kütahiya and a former imperial *kapucibasi*. [26] Dervish Hüseyn ("Hyso") wed locally and found some employment for his knowledge of chancery Turkish which the local administrator, like most untravelled Epirote Moslems of those times, may not have known. His son, Mustafa (Meço Hyso), grew up to become one of the most ferocious aghas of the district, leading a band of nearly one hundred men in plundering forays as far south as Acarnania and Thessaly. There he met determined resistance only from the *armatolos* Boukouvalas, for whose descendents Ali was to nurse a lively hatred. Beqir and Muhtar, Meço Hyso's two sons, both adopted the title "bey" from their mother's side. The oldest, Beqir, died in Tepeleni leaving a son, Islam. Muhtar, as previously noted, was killed in the siege of Corfu, leaving a son, Veli, and two daughters: Marjam, who married in Tepeleni, and Ajse, who wed Ismail Bey Klisura.

Along with the shadowy title of "bey," Beqir and Muhtar inherited equally dubious feudal rights over the Christian villages of the Rhiza of Argyrocastron—Giates, Kakozi, Kargianni, Khoundekouki, Labovo ("of Zappas"), Terbouki, Lekli and Chormovo. When Islam Bey, as senior descendent and technically the family head, denied his cousin Veli a right to this inheritance, Veli, like his grandfather, turned to banditry. Then, one night, Veli suddenly descended on Tepeleni, murdered Islam in his bed, and kidnapped Islam's widow, Qarka, and her two sons, Ismail and Tahir. He married the widow and took over his cousin's estate. Veli also took a second wife, Hanko, daughter of Zejnel Bey Konitsa whose ancestor, Lytfi Konitsa, had been pasha of Yannina from 1550 to 1590. When Veli died, Hanko feared his enemies would attack her and her two children to assert the rights of Qarko and Islam Bey's orphans.

---

[24] On January 11, 1801. The lament for Kyra Phrosyne and the seventeen will be found in Emile Legrand,*Recueil de Chansons Populaires Grecques*, Paris, 1873, p. 118, (Greek text, French tr.), and in nearly every modern Greek folksong anthology.

[25] Bekkerus, *op. cit.*, p. 219.

[26] One of the Sultan's forty five official doorkeepers.

Her fears that they would attempt to do away with her and her son, Ali, born in 1744, and daughter, Shahinica, born in 1750, were quite real.

She prevented that in short order by having the unwanted trio murdered. Then, fearing their partisans' revenge, she fled to a fortified castle overlooking the Christian village of Kargianni. But she and her children were not safe even there, for the Moselm aghas of Gardiki disputed her overlordship of the Rhiza. They did not hinder the *armatoloi* of the larger villages, such as Chormovo and Lekli, from defying Hanko and the youthful Ali.

From time immemorial, bandits had been lynched on the great Tree of Judgment, an immense plane tree at the pass where the highways of Berati, Valona and Tepeleni meet. It was under this unpleasant reminder that Ali, on his way one day to assert his seignorial rights in the reluctant villages, was waylaid and captured. The leader of the band, the son of Father Costas Demas of Chormovo, Demetrios Pappademas, told Ali that if he wanted his inheritance he could try and take it from his foes in Tepeleni who would sooner give him short shrift. With this warning, Pappademas, who was nicknamed "Sergeant Priest," (Tsaoush Prifti), told Ali to return whence he had come.

When he became pasha of Yannina, the no longer youthful miscreant's memory recalled the humiliation of long ago—and he acted. One of his first acts as pasha in 1788 was to surround Chormovo, where he had as many of the Chormovans as did not flee or accept Islam massacred and their women and girls sold into slavery. Tsaoush Prifti, who eluded Ali at first, was captured near the Moslem village of Zouliates by Yusuf Arapi, the pasha's savage lieutenant. He was brought bound to the Christian village of Nokovon. At the village's outskirts was the mill of John Lekas, who had the misfortune of having been born in Chormovo. Nearby was a characteristic wayside shrine. First Lekas himself was tied to his own millstone and ground to death. Then Tsaoush Prifti, who was many years the pasha's senior, was given the traditional choice of embracing either Islam or death. Ali knew what the reply would be and relished the fate he had prepared for the old man. He watched with evident enjoyment as Yusuf first dragged Tsaoush Prifti before the shrine and multilated him and then spitted him to make an obscene barbeque.

The sons of Chormovo who fled, together with the Souliotes and the Chimarriotes, wrote a golden page in the annals of the Greek War of Independence. Chormovo, resettled by Moslems from the Lab village of Golemi, is Moslem today. But what happened there 180 years ago is an unperishable part of the oral tradition of the people who are still Albania's captives.[27]

[27] Among the heroes of 1821, Greece recalls the names of the Chormovans Kostas Chormovas (Lagoumtzis), Demos Lioulias, Anastasios Chormovas, Evangelos Dalamangas and many others.

7.

Ali Pasha kur qe djalë
në Hormovë e kish inanë
përmbi Çaush Kapetane.
Kush qe në kotë e parë?
Hormovitë kordhëtarë!
Që Hormovë e tatëpjetë
kapetan seç jeshë vetë
me njëqind e pesëdhjetë.
S'fala Turk mbë këtë jetë!

N'atë zemanin e parë,
Hormovitë kordhëtarë
tetëqind qenë me pallë.
Tetëqind me pallë qenë,
kishë zaptuar dervenë
Beratë, Vlorë e Tepelenë.

Tepelena është karshi;
kreu egjërsin Ali!
Në Rrap i Muaqemenë
dërgojnë mbi Ali Benë:
"Të vi poshtë në Tepelenë,
se xhindet muarnë dhenë."

Shkrova kart' e t'a dërgova;
me lotë syvet e shkrova:
"Kapetan, o, Çaush Prifti,
ç'deshi ti të Hormoviti?
Mos na shkoni nga Zhulati,
se na sheh Isuf Arapi."

O, Çaush, o, yll, o, dritë,
të kërkojnë Hormovitë.
Të qajnë motrat e zeza,
të qajnë derë me derë,
të qajnë krua me krua:
"Kini parë, a s'kini parë
të pjekë i biri t'anë?
Nën-o moj, e zeza nënë,
del e shih Çaushin tënë,
tek e pjekinë ndë lëmë."

Dolli zonja m'u tek muri:
'Shihni si piqet kahuri;
si e pjek Isuf Arapi
i pikon dhe dhjame cjapi."

Kapetan Çaush Hormova,
ndënë konismë të drodha.
Në derë të zezit Lekë,
flet ay Veziri vetë:
"Ashkolsun Isuf Arapi,
ç'të erdhka dorë kasapi!

Kapetan Çaush Hormova,

Ali Pasha when a youth
Had a feud with Chormovo,
With Captain Tsaoush.
Who in vainglory were first?
The Chormovan swordsmen!
From Chormovo and beyond,
Sole Captain was I then
With a hundred and fifty men.
Beholden to no Turk was I in this life!

In that season of yore,
The Chormovan swordsmen
Were eight hundred armed with sabres.
Eight hundred with sabres were they
When they siezed the highways
Of Berati, Avlona and Tepeleni.

Opposite lies Tepeleni;
It produced Ali the brute!
At the Plane Tree of Judgment,
They gave Ali Bey an order:
"Get yourself down to Tepeleni,
For Demons have siezed the land."

I wrote a letter and dispatched it;
I wrote it with tears in my eyes:
"Oh Captain Tsaoush Prifti,
What do you wish of the Chormovan?
Let us pass not by Zouliates,
For Yusuf Arapi will see us."

Oh Tsaoush, oh star, oh light,
You are sought by the Chormovans.
Your blackened sisters lament you,
Lament you from door to door,
Lament you from fountain to fountain:
"Have you seen or have you not
How a son roasts the father?
Oh mother, blackened mother,
Go forth to see our Tsaoush,
How he is roasted by the mill."

The lady went forth to the wall:
"See you how the infidel is roasted;
As Yusuf Arapi roasts him
He drips and the goat's fat spills."

Captain Tsaoush of Chormovo,
'Neath the shrine they castrated you.
By blackened Lekas' door
Speaks the Vizier himself:
"Well done, Yusuf Arapi,
Accomplished with a butcher's skill!

Captain Tsaoush of Chormovo,

me gjithë farën lëftova!	I have fought with all your tribe!
O, Çaush, more Çaush,	Oh Tsaoush, hey you Tsaoush,
zëmra t'u dogji në prush!	I've burnt your heart on embers!
Çaush Prift, Çaush Hormova,	Tsaoush Prifti, Tsaoush Chormovan,
dhjamë e dyllë të pikova,	I've spilled your fat and tallow,
ty dot besën s'ta ndërrova!"	Yet your faith I could not change!

Orphaned by his father's death in 1753, Ali never ceased to acknowledge the debt he owed to his mother's upbringing, and this debt is written in the blood of those who were to die at his hands. An Albanian Moslem folksong links Hanko and her infamous son in his deeds that "destroyed all the Morea."[28]

8.

Hanko kur polle Alinë,	Hanko, when she gave birth to Ali,
Hanko Pash' e Hanko nure,	Hanko Pasha and Hanko bright,
ndriti bota vetëtimë!	Lit up the world with the glow!
Ali Pasha Tepelenë,	Ali Pasha of Tepeleni,
gjarpëri që piu dhenë,	The earth-drinking serpent,
bëri fet gjithë Morenë!	Destroyed all of the Morea!

His struggle with the aghas of Gardiki over the rights to exploit the Rhiza came to a head while Ali was away on one of his bandit forays. One day in August, 1762, Hanko and Shahinica were captured in a Gardikiote raid on Kargianni. Their castle was plundered and set afire, and they were carried off with the booty to Gardiki. The loot was piled high in the village square for distribution, while the proud Hanko and her daughter were mockingly asked by the Gardikiotes to tell them the cost of each item. One of the Gardikiotes, Haxhi Aga, brother of Dost Bey, perhaps was moved by pity, but more likely troubled by possible retribution. One night, he took the two women secretly to Giates, another Christian village of Rhiza which was subject to Hanko and her son, and there released them. Since the castle in Kargianni was destroyed, Hanko built a second one at Giates.

When the Gardikiotes learned of Hanko's flight, they attempted to pursue. Once free, however, Hanko was able to gather her retainers for a fight and the Gardikiotes, alarmed, retired without giving battle. The incident was another affront Ali was not to forget, but one less easy to avenge, since the Gardikiotes were not *kahurs*[29], but Moslems. The time

---

[28] *Morea* is a term properly applied only to the Peloponnese. In Albanian colloquial usage, however, it is often extended to include the whole of southern Greece.

[29] *kahur:* infidel, a word used so often as a Moslem epithet for Christian that, in occasional colloquial usage, it was used by the Christians of themselves. The Moslems of Epirus, who never lost sight completely of the fact that their ancestors were apostates or forced converts from Greek Orthodoxy, often chided each other with the pejorative "bir i kahurit," (son of an infidel!)

of revenge was not to come until 24 years after Ali became pasha of Yannina and only ten years before his death at the age of 88. But when it came, it was with a thoroughness that would have done credit to a general in the Nazi SS. Since Ali was bent on gathering all power into his gory hands, he was forced, during his long rule, into constant conflicts not only with rayas[30], but with the petty beys and aghas whose local tyranny both preceded and succeeded his own. An expedition in February 1812 forced the aghas and beys of Argyrocastron to knuckle under, but some fled to well-fortified lairs in Gardiki and Ali had the excuse he sought.[31] After an uneven battle, the Gardikiotes surrendered and were disarmed. Seventy-two Gardikiotes, including Demir Dosti and Ismail Delvina, were tied in pairs and led on a long march to Yannina where they were executed. The rest were led, on March 15, 1812, to a walled inn at the edge of a valley called Valiare, a pasturage located directly across from Argyrocastron and at the foot of a hill called Çajupi. Like a herd of sheep, they were driven into the courtyard of the inn and the stout gates were shut. Ali's soldiers then took places atop the wall and fired upon the unarmed Gardikiotes, most of them women and children, until not a living thing was left. The reference in the following song to Kakodiki refers to a Christian village whose population in 1908 was 460 and which was a çiflik or latifundium of the Gardikiote Moslems.

9.

Të hani i Valaresë	At the inn of Valiare
i bir i Hanko kahpesë	The son of Hanko the whore
ua bëri me të pabesë;	Took them in with treachery;
vrau shtatëqint e pesë.	He shot seven hundred and five.
Mun të han i Valaresë,	About the inn of Valiare,
plumbat vininë si vese.	The shot fell like dew.
Mbë batare i vrau djemtë	With firing squad they shot the children
mbyllur ndë hobor si dhentë.	Locked in the courtyard like sheep.
O, bubu, burrat t'anë,	Oh, what woe befell our men,
ç'të keqë me sy që panë!	What evils have mine eyes beheld!
Kardhiqotë gunë dhirë,	Gardikiotes in goatskin fleeces,
ku e latë trimërinë?	Where did you lose your warriors?
Kardhiqotë vergjë-vergjë,	Gardikiotes line upon line,
ca me guna, ca me sherqë;	Some with fleeces, some with capotes,
Janinë i shpunë të gjallë;	To Yannina alive were brought;
me të pabesë ç'i vranë.	With treachery they were slain.

[30] raya: human cattle, a term applied from one end of the Ottoman Empire to the other to designate Christians.

[31] Another Greek ballad accurately describes the battle that followed. See A. Passow, Popularia Carmina Graeciae Recentioris, Leipzig 1860, p. 160.

Kakodhiq, pse s'nxorre lule?	Kakodiki, why don't you blossom?
Apo mban zi për të zotë,	Do you don mourning for your masters,
për të zestë Kardhiqotë	For your lords the Gardikiotes
që van e s'u kthyen dotë?	Who went to return no more?
O, të zezë Kardhiqotë,	Oh, ye blackened Gardikiotes,
vat' e më s'u kthyet dotë!	You left to return no more!

When Moslem as well as Christian villages became the objects of his forays, his fellow beys called upon Kurd Pasha of Berati, who had been named *dervedat nazir* by the Porte in 1760, to protect them. Kurd Pasha's men succeeded in cornering and capturing Ali in a village in the Pogoni district and took him before Kurd in Berati. Mistaking earnest criminality for youthful high spirits, Kurd unexpectedly forgave Ali who soon returned to Tepeleni as Kurd Pasha's protegé. Ali saw a marital alliance in Kurd's daughter, Marjam, but, instead she married Ibrahim Bey Vlorë. This was just as well, in view of the fate of the woman who did become his first wife, Emine, daughter of Kaplan Pasha Delvina, governor of Argyrocastron. The Tepelenian's immediate reaction to Kurd's rejection of the marital alliance was a rash return to banditry, a decision neither prospects nor the number of his men justified. He attacked the Christian village of Lekli, nominally subordinate to him, but was beaten off. Pursued by Kurd's men with a bounty of 5,000 piastres on his head, Ali took refuge in the home of a Lab named Belushi in the village of Lekdushi. There, abandoned by nearly all his stalwarts, he came upon a scheme. He had two of his remaining supporters, Lek Duro and Skendo Buja, wrap his clothes about a sheep that was run through. The bloody clothes were taken to Kurd Pasha as proof that Ali was dead, and Ali thereupon collected the reward and fled to the protection of Kurd's enemy, Kaplan Pasha. The aged Kaplan Pasha was the grandson of Aslan Pasha II of Yannina. Aslan, who ruled Yannina from 1702 to 1720, was killed suppressing a Christian revolt in Arta and was entombed in the still existing mosque that he erected.[32]

Aslan's daughter had married the pasha of Argyrocastron where his son, Mustafa, also settled. Since the pasha was without sons, he adopted Mustafa's son, Kaplan, who in time succeeded to the pashalik. Ali not only fled to Kaplan's protection, but managed as well what he had been unable to do with Kurd—contract a marital alliance. He wed Kaplan's daughter, Emine, in Argyrocastron where his two sons, Muhtar and Veli, were born. In addition, his sister married Kaplan's son, Ali Delvina, by whom she had a daughter, Asimbe. Kaplan, his son and Emine herself were all to become Ali's victims. When pasha of Yannina, Ali was to

---

[32] The Mosque of Aslan Pasha, overlooking the lake of Yannina, is now the Municipal Museum.

shoot Emine himself in a fit of rage. But first he destroyed her family in this wise:

When the "Orlov Uprising" took place from one end of Greece to the other, Kaplan was secretly denounced to the Porte by his son-in-law for allegedly entering treasonable negotiations with the rebellious Chimarriotes. Kaplan was enticed to Monastir (Bitolj) and there beheaded. But Ali was cheated of the prize. The pashalik went to Ali Delvina and Ali then urged a half-brother, Sylejman, to kill him and claim it himself. When Sylejman agreed to do so, Ali retired to Tepeleni after having patched up another truce with Kurd Pasha. He did not have long to wait. He returned to Argyrocastron to console his widowed sister—and marry her off to the murderer by whom she was to bear two sons, Elmaz Pasha and Edhem Bey Libohova, father of the wealthy Malik Pasha. To the disappointment of the conspirators, the pashalik went first to Mustafa Aga Koka and then, in 1775, to his rival, Selim Bey Mustafa. Selim Pasha was a peaceful but foolish man. He took Ali into his confidence, was denounced by Ali to the Porte for alleged treasonable relations with Venice and was decapitated in 1778.

Selim was lured to his death when Ali feigned illness at the home of a fellow conspirator and the pasha was prevailed upon to pay him a sick-bed call from which he never returned. Ali subsequently fled with Selim's two sons, Shahin and Mustafa Bey, to Tepeleni. Mustafa Bey defeated Ali's renewed intrigues through his Constantinople agents by escaping the fate reserved for him, reaching Argyrocastron and succeeding in being named pasha in his dead father's stead.

Meanwhile, in 1784, Kurd Pasha died and was succeeded by Ibrahim Pasha Vlorë. Ali may have been tempted to return to banditry, but intrigue had shown him an easier way to gain his ends. The klepht-ridden pashalik of Trikkala was vacant and Ali's agents, for once had a good argument in persuading the Porte that "it takes a thief to catch one." They managed to procure for him not only the pashalik, but the title of *dervedat nazir* as well in 1785.

THE "LION" ROARS
(1788-1803)

Ali now had both means and power to hold out prospects to his fellow Labs, and 4,000 choice cutthroats accompanied him to his Thessalian pashalik. There Ali was able to put down a few klephts and bag enough severed heads to provide visible proof to his patrons in Stamboul of his energy.

Meanwhile, the Vilayet of Yannina had fallen on evil days. The incompetent Sylejman Pasha III was beheaded by the Porte's orders. His aunt and widow—a sister of one of his predecessors—found his constable and former coffee brewer more to her taste, which may have been the real cause of his abrupt end. The widow Ajse then married Ali Zot, the Argyrocastran ex-coffee brewer, who at least had good looks—if nothing more—in his favor. Ajse's mismanagement and the Yanniote beys' general dissatisfaction while Ali Zot was away at war with the Turks against the Russians in the Danubian Principalities, led to a complete administrative breakdown in 1788. This was Ali's chance to surround Yannina with his troops. When this served to unite Ajse's interests with the opposing beys, Ali drove a new wedge by proposing marriage to Zilhako, the widow of a former pasha's son. In the confusion that followed, Ali moved fast. In the dead of night, he and his followers were rowed from the lake's opposite shore at Perama to Yannina's citadel. Ajse disputed the city with him, but Ali produced a forged imperial *firman* naming him pasha.

He then took firm control of both the city and the province and awaited word of the negotiations—well-oiled with bribes—of his Constantinople agents with the Janissary aghas and the Divan. The confirmation soon came and Ali became ruler of both Epirus and Thessaly. His domains, through what he was able to seize or buy, came in time to include even the Peloponnese where, for a time, the Pasha of Tripolitsa and his unofficial viceroy was his son Veli. But he, like his predecessors, was to have his troubles with the Chimarriotes, the Souliotes and the myriad-headed Greek hydra, the klephts. Out of these conflicts was to arise the birth of modern Greece.

In 1798, (the following song prefers the "round" number 1800), Ali entered into an agreement with the French in Corfu to allow him to send a force through the straits to the small harbor of Loukovo. From there, during Holy Week, he attacked and set fire to Nivitsa Boubari and St. Basil.[33]

The song refers to Memush Kumbulla, an otherwise unknown agent of the pasha, who apparently brought him tidings of the Chimarriotes' resistance and met his death at their hands. It also refers to the *armatolos* Karaiskakes who ultimately emerged as commanding general of the Greek revolutionary forces in Thessaly. It would have him serving Ali's son, Veli, in the Peloponnese at the time. This, however, is inaccurate since Veli was not appointed Pasha of Tripolitsa until 1807. A further somewhat indelicate reference is made to the pasha's private predelictions. A biographer tells us, "In his harem were enclosed about 300 Christian, Moslem, Albanian and Circassian concubines while, in the private apartments of the seraglios of both himself and his sons were disposed numerous youthful, goodlooking ganymedes."[34]

10.

Kur qe tetëqind seneja,
dërgoj Memush kahpeja:
"Ali Pasha, ngreu, eja,
se ngriti krye rajeja."

When it was the year Eighteen Hundred,
Memush the whore sent word:
"Ali Pasha, get up, come,
For the *raya* lifts his head."

"Falu, o, Shën Vasil i shkretë!"
"S'falemi sa jemi vetë!
Ç'e pandeh, o, Ali Pasha?
Mos jemi çupa nga Narta
edhe djemt nga Gjirokastra
të loç ti me 'ta nga nata!

"Barren Saint Basil, submit!"
"We do not bow while we're alive!
What think you, oh Ali Pasha?
We're not the girls from Arta
And the boys from Argyrocastron
Like those you play with at night!

"Ne jemi kapetanata,
Major Dhima kordhëshpata,
Spiro Buti qafë gjati."

"We are the captaincies,
The swordsman Major Demas,
The long-necked Spiros Boutis."

Thotë Kapetan Sokrati:
"Të mbaj, burra, të mbaj,
se u trëmb Ali Pashaj."

Spake Captain Socrates:
"Hold fast, men, hold fast,
For Ali Pasha trembles."

Dërgoj të Veli Agaj,
Veli Bej Tripolicani,
të dërgon Karajshkaqin.

He sends to Veli Agha,
Veli Bey the Tripolitsan,
To send him Karaiskakis.

Gati ia bëri ordhinë,
asqer dymbëdhjetë mijë,

Ready he made his horde,
An army of twelve thousand,

[33] *AC*, p. 41.

[34] Aravantinos, *op. cit.*, pp. 436, 437.

të rrethosnin Shën Vasinë,	To surround Saint Basil,
Nivicën dhe Bubarinë.	Nivitsa and Boubari.
Erdh' Karajshkua Delvinë	Karaiskakis came to Delvino
të prëmtën ndë të gdhirë.	On Friday at daybreak.
Zu e mëson talim ordhinë.	He began to drill his horde.
Ra dielli mbë saba,	When the sun arose at dawn,
zuri kulat të mëdha.	He seized the great towers.
Vuri dylbinë e pa:	He raised binoculars and spied:
"Mba vesh, o, Ali Pasha,	"Give heed, oh Ali Pasha,
ndë divan rrinë ca gra.	Some women arive in the sitting room.
Seç qënka e mesmja!"	The middle one is so pretty!"
Edh' Ali Pashaj i tha:	And Ali Pasha said to him:
"U! Pa të shohç ay q'e ka?"	"Oh, don't you see who has her?"
Edhe nesërmet kur pa,	And the next day when he looked,
Memush Kumbulla u vra;	Memush Kumbulla was slain;
Koka ndë ferra i ra!	His head fell in the brambles!

Chimarra had been broken before and had arisen again to haunt the overlords of Epirus. Many years after Ali Pasha was gone, the resistance of the Greek Chimarriotes was to manifest itself as if Ali had never been. Nonetheless, Ali slew many of them and many others fled to the haven of Corfu to await the passing of the annihilating wind that swept over their Acroceraunian Mountains. They could see the fires of their abandoned hearths from the heights of Corfu and remember the paths they had trod and the springs from which they had drunk. Thus was born from their anonymous bards the following plaint:

11.

Himar', e zeza Himarë,	Chimarra, black Chimarra,
njëqind e njëzet kambanë,	One Hundred and twenty churchbells,
o, ju kambanat, pse s'biri?	Bells, why ring ye not?
A po trëmbi nga veziri?	Are you frightened of the vizier?
Biri, moj të shkreta, biri!	Ring, ye barren ones, ring!
Shokë, ç'më ka zënë malli	Companions, a yearning takes me
për sejir të Barbakajit	For a stroll by Barbaka
dhe për ujë të Fitajit!	And for Phita's water!

Another thorn in the tyrant's side from which was to bloom the rose of Greek independence was the mountain "republic" of Souli, composed chiefly of the villages of Souli, Kiapha, Avarikos and Samoniva. Set in wooded hills well-guarded by masters in the hard art of guerrilla warfare, Souli was inhabited by folk speaking both Albanian and Greek who had gathered from many parts of Epirus to this natural stronghold. Some had fled from as far north as the villages of Labëria when that area swung over to Islam. Others had come from other nearby Thesprotian villages, fleeing the harsh rule of the beys and aghas of Philiates and Margariti.[35]

In times of peril, the Souliotes could count upon the Christian villages of the surrounding territory to join them, but they themselves made up an aristocracy of valor, entry into which could only be obtained by conspicuous bravery. Tales were told of the Souliote womenfolk's custom of yielding first place at the communal well to the wife of the bravest warrior. Then too, the women were unlike the comparatively shy wives of the other mountain villages of Greece, and were as used to arms as the men and often took part in skirmishes as a group apart. And, if the men were justly proud and often contentious, the women were the arbiters of their differences. When these flared, no man dared intervene between disputants for fear of accusation by one side of favoring the other. But a woman's judgment was accepted in respectful silence by all, since no warrior was so unmanly as to argue publicly with a woman.

Byron prophesied better than he knew then when he wrote of these Homeric types beside whom he was to fight and die in Greece's war for freedom at Missolonghi:

> Fill high the bowl with Samian wine!
> On Suli's rock, and Parga's shore,
> Exists the remnant of a line
> Such as the Doric mothers bore;
> And there, perhaps, some seed is sown,
> The Heracleidan blood might own.[36]

It was with these freeborn sons of the Epirote hills, not far from Yannina itself, that Ali, in the fourth year of his misrule, began what promised to be a minor campaign of subjugation. Instead, it was an 18-year war in which some 30,000 of his best troops were to find themselves at a disadvantage against 5,000 defiant Souliotes. Ali began with the usual overtures of peace and promises of special consideration as the price of Souliote submission. If the Souliotes would but become tributary, if they would but bow their foreheads low like other *rayas,* accept Ali's tax-gatherers and a garrison of Albanian Moslems, their tranquility was assured. But the Souliotes told Ali that their freedom was only to be won and preserved in the only coin they recognized—that of self-sacrifice and resistance. Accordingly, Ali gathered his forces and hurled them against the Souliotes who had defied his predecessors in eight previous attempts.

What happened before Ali's eyes as he watched from a distance sent him back to Yannina in impotent rage, crying aloud "Ububu! Mëndet

---

[35] Memories of this rule were revived during World War II when the Nazis' Albanian gauleiter Xhemil Dino and his brother Nuri set up the "liberated" territory of "Çamërija." Some Albanian super-nationalists dream of it yet by claiming the territory as an Albanian irredenta. *Vide AC* pp. 142, 143, also Th. G. Papamanoles, *Flameswept Epirus,* Athens, 1945.

[36] George Gordon, Lord Byron, *The Poet's Song; The Isles of Greece.*

Allah," "Woe is me! God have mercy." It was said that he withdrew to
his harem and would speak with no man for a fortnight. Many of Ali's
troops fled to the huts of Christian peasants nearby, quartering themselves there overnight to escape their pursuers. Few arose in the morning.
Among those who took part in this successful first encounter with Ali's
forces were 300 Souliote women under the fierce command of Moscho,
the wife of the equally outstanding Captain Photos Tzavellas. In prefacing
the song that follows, it is fitting to yield place to one of Ali's contemporary arch-foes, "Christopher Perrhaebus the Thessalian," actually
Chrysaphes Chatzivasiliou of Siatista, Macedonia.

The sole surviving companion of the poet and revolutionary martyr
Rhigas Pheraios, child of the Enlightenment, agent of the Revolution in
Parga and director of the secret Friendly Society in Epirus, none more
qualified can be found. But a few years after the events, Perrhaebus
wrote: [37]

> Such was the glorious conclusion reached by the Souliotes' ninth war
> and Ali Pasha's first against them, about which we have gathered
> information by exact examination of various participants and from the
> Briton's history. [38]
>
> Ali's troops, on one hand, were no fewer than 10,000. Those of the
> Souliotes, on the other, were no more than two. This battle took
> place in June 1792. Of the Turko-Albanians, over 2,000 were
> slaughtered, not including the unknown wounded and those sacrificed
> by the peasants. Of the Souliotes, 74 fell and 97 were wounded.
>
> It is neither superfluous nor unpleasant, I believe, to set down herein
> the song then composed about this war, as an accompaniment to the
> accounts: [39]

12.

Tri zogëza po rrinin	Three birds were sitting
ndë qaf të Shëndeliut.	On Saint Elias' ridge.
Njera shikon Janinën,	One looks toward Yannina,
tjetra Kakosulin.	The other to Kakosouli.
E treta, e më e mirëza,	The third, best of the lot,
po logoris e thotë:	Laments the while and says:

[37] Christopher Perrhaebus, *Complete Works*, Athens, 1956, pp. 91, 92. The text
of the quoted prefatory remarks is from the 3rd ed. of his *History of Souli and
Parga*, 2 Vols., Athens, 1857.

[38] William Eton, *Survey of the Turkish Empire*, London, 1798.

[39] Because the above Albanophone Epirote version tallies nearly verbatim with the
most commonly found Greek version and is unrhymed, a characteristic rare in
Albanian verse but common in Greek, it would appear that what we have is an
anonymous Northern Epirote translation of a song known from one end of continental Greece to the other. It is a rare Greek folksong anthology that omits it.
Among others, see Polites, *op. cit.*, pp. 14, 15. Besides the above, there are other
songs in what constitutes a veritable modern Greek cycle relating to the Souliote
struggle against Ali Pasha. It would not be amiss for the reader who can compare
to include here the Greek text most nearly identical with the above. See Appendix A.

"U mblodhë Shqipëtarët
i u turre Kakosulit.
Me tre bajrakë shkuan,
të tre radhë mbë radhë.
Njeri qe i Myftar Pashajt,
tjetri i Meço Bonos.
I treti, e më i bukuri,
ishte e Zylyftarit."

Një prifteresh po thrret
kah një breg i lartë:
"Ku jini, djemt e Boçarit,
o, djemte Kuçonikës?
Turqit na mbuluanë,
duan të na robërojnë;
në Tepelenë të na shpien,
besën të na ndërrojnë."

E Kuçonika sokëllin
që atje nga Avariku:
"Moj prifteresh, mos u trëmb,
as mos e shko ndë mëndje.
Tani të shohç luftën,
dyfeqe kapetanësh,
se qysh lëftojnë trimat,
trimat e Kakosulit."

"The Albanians have gathered
Round about Kakosouli.
With three standards went they forth,
The three of them close together.
One is that of Muhtar Pasha,
The other of Metso Bonos.
The third, most beautiful of all
Was that of Zylyftari.

The wife of a priest summoned forth
From a high hill's cliff:
"Where are you, sons of Botsaris,
Oh sons of Koutsonikas?
The Turks have surrounded us,
They desire to enslave us;
To Tepeleni send us off,
From our faith to change us."

And Koutsonikas gave a shout
There out of Avarikos:
"Fear not you, wife of the priest,
Let it not be brought to mind.
Now you will behold the war,
The muskets of the captains,
How the warriors make war,
The braves of Kakosouli.

It cost the pasha many years, many battles and much blood to subdue Souli. His argument was a good one—a blockade of Souli which the Souliotes, however brave, could not withstand forever. This did not escape some of the Souliotes who had fought Ali the hardest in the early stages of the contest. Besides, as the war dragged out, what had been rivalries between Souliote captains was bound to become exacerbated to open hostility.

The pasha's foil was Pilios Gousis, a spy who insinuated himself into the circle of Captain George Botsaris and slyly played upon both the aging captain's fear of the future and his rivalry with the clan of Tzavellas. Soon Botsaris, who had led the resistance, began to preach acceptance of Ali's terms to end further bloodshed. When public scorn was his answer, Botsaris had little choice but to take himself and his faction out of Souli and capitulate to Ali, who was determined to destroy him in a more terrible way than physical extermination. Botsaris was ordered to give proof of the sincerity of his surrender by joining Ali's forces in the assault on Souli. At Radovouni, along with Ali's men, Botsaris and his traitors fought against the Souliotes who, under Captains Tzavellas, Dangles, Photomaras and Karabinas were again triumphant. The last shred of his moral prestige gone, Botsaris suffered the reproaches of his own son Tousas. When he could bear the burden of conscience no longer, he took poison and died. Ali's impossible war with the Souliotes continued.

Botsaris' name would have deserved to be ranked with Ephialtes, the betrayer of Thermopylae, had the story of his family ended at this point. Instead, it is synonymous in modern Greek history with glorious self-sacrifice for God and country, and the man who was to redeem the name and exemplify these virtues were George Botsaris' grandson Marcos.

Besieged but unvanquished, the Souliotes' position grew even more impossible and only one hope remained. If Ali wanted Souli, they would abandon it to him—without the Souliotes. Corfu, occupied by the Russians since 1799, offered more than a haven. If Ali let them pass, they would make use of the opportunity to prepare for another day's fight. The next Russo-Turkish war—there was always a Russo-Turkish war—might return them to Souli in triumph as the spearhead of an Orthodox Christian army of liberation. The hope was a fugitive one, but little else remained for them to believe in. Thus, under truce, a Souliote delegation met with Ali on Dec. 12, 1803, and sealed a pact permitting the mass evacuation. A lone dissenter, the monk-priest Samuel, held aloof from the pact of despair. Souli's defenders left their mountaintop fortress of Koungi to the birds of prey and Samuel alone remained. As the Moslem Albanian garrison entered the fort's tower where the powder magazine was kept, Samuel crossed himself, hurled a firebrand and Souli, defiant to the last, passed into immortality.

One group of Souliotes marched to the port of Preveza while a second took the more northerly route to the sea at Parga. Both were harried on that sorrowful anabasis by Ali's forces for whom a pledge of honor to infidels never stayed the hand of plunder and rapine.

A party of one hundred women and children were cut off near the monastery of Zalongo where they resisted until capture seemed imminent. As the Moslems closed in, the women seized their children and joined hands in a frenzied dance of death, throwing themselves off a cliff until not one remained. With these terrible yet sacred memories, the Souliotes arrived in Corfu proposing to continue their fight in the Russian ranks. Tzavellas accepted a commission in the Tsar's army, but Russian promises soon wore thin and he turned in his commission in disgust.

The hats and trousers worn by the Souliotes in their exile became a symbol of their alienation from their native soil—to end only when they could cast them aside for their own kilts and fezzes. Poverty, illness and old age thinned their ranks, but the children succeeded their fathers and the Souliotes did return. And when they touched their native soil again on Dec. 12, 1820—seventeen years to the day their exile began—they were clad in no foreign uniform, but in their own well-worn fustanellas.

Somewhere on Corfu, a homesick and bewildered Souliote soldier must have been the first to sing this song.

13.

Ti, more Foto Xhavella,	You, oh Photos Tzavellas,
seç na bërë me kapella?	Why do you have us wearing hats?
seç u prem e seç u vramë?	Why were we wounded and why were we
Sulin e shkret' ku e lamë?	slain?
	Where did we leave barren Souli?
Ali Pashajt ia dhamë,	To Ali Pasha we gave it,
nat' e ditë rrim e qajmë.	Night and day we sit and cry.
Fati në Korfuz na hodhi;	Fate has cast us upon Corfu;
zumë dorë të Moskovi.	We have grasped the Muscovite's hand.
Me Moskov lidhem kuvëndin	With the Muscovite we've sealed a pact
të vemi e të marrim vëndin.	To go and take back our country.
Vemi e vdesim ndë dhënë tënë,	Let us go and die on our soil
atje tek e patem thënë.	There where it's written we must.
Vdesim me dyfek në dorë	Let us die with a musket in hand
si dhendurë me Kurorë!	Like bridegrooms wearing crowns!

The hopes of the mainland Greek exiles on Corfu grew dimmer as the Ionian Islands became French in 1807 and British in 1809—the latter occupation lasting until 1863. Each of these occupying powers, in turn, courted the goodwill of the tyrant of Epirus.

While the exiles' hopes were not met in the least by the French occupation, it did afford some protection to Parga on the seacoast which remained an enclave under whatever flag flew over Corfu. Moreover, through the existence of a Greek mercantile class in the West, a good part of it drawn from emigrated sons of Epirus, the ideas of the French Revolution began to penetrate Greek circles even in the court of Ali Pasha.

The British occupation, however humane for the islanders themselves, dashed even the solace provided by the continued existence of a Parga on the mainland by sale of that enclave to Ali in 1819.[40]

The myth of Russian intervention, however, died hard among the Epirote, Thessalian and Aetolo-Acarnanian freedom fighters exiled on Corfu or fighting in their hills.

In the summer of 1814, the battle of Borodino had been fought, Napoleon had been expelled from Russia and the Russian emperor, along with his Prussian and British allies, had made his triumphant entry into Paris. On June 30 that year, through the good offices of their countryman Count John Capodistrias, the Russian foreign minister[41], the Greeks submitted a memorandum to Tsar Alexander I in Vienna. This was another, perhaps the last, of the pitiable manifesti of the Greeks begging the Russians to come to their aid. Among the signers of this memorandum were Colonel Strates Ghikas of Chimarra; Majors Spiros Doukas of St.

---

[40] See *AC*, p. 41.

[41] See *AC*, p. 46.

Basil, Stephan Tzakos of Chimarra and Athanasios Aïvasiotes of St. Basil; Lieutenants Vieros Doukas and Alexis Soulos of St. Basil and Stephan Caesares of Loukovo and Father Athanasius of St. Basil, chaplain.[42]

But if the Tsar of All the Russias and founder of the Holy Alliance was to show the Greeks no encouragement, the secret society founded on Russian soil that year by three Greek merchants, two of them Epirotes, was to give birth to new hopes.[43] These hopes could only be realized when Ali's sun had begun to set.

[42] See Mammopoulos, *op. cit.,* Vol. II, p. 55.

[43] See *AC*, p. 43. Also Angelos N. Papakostas, *"Friendly Society Members from Northern Epirus" in *Neos Koubaras*, 1961, pp. 66-72.

THE "LION" IS SLAIN
(1804-1822)

Because the downfall and death struggle of the "Lion of Yannina" were catalysts releasing long-suppressed forces, the context within which these events occurred is of no little importance. When Ali took power, the storming of the Bastille to the cry of "Liberty, Fraternity and Equality" was but a year away. When he ceased to be, Louis XVIII was perched precariously on the battered throne of France and Metternich was calling the tune of European reaction.

The interim saw the world turned upside down. The year the French throne toppled also witnessed the passing of Sultan Abdul Hamid I and the girding of the sword of Osman by Sultan Selim III. Selim and his advisors might view the revolutions of Washington and the French Republicans as a vain attempt to assert the equality of the donkey with the donkey driver, but they were well aware of the dangers.

As yet, the dangers for the *muminin,* the faithful who saw the "Padishah" as the God-ordained successor of the Prophet Mohammed himself, were nil. And there were no Turkish intellectuals as yet who yearned to pin a tricolor cockade to their turbans. But in the Balkans, as if the close proximity of Orthodox Russia were not enough, Revolutionary France now put in an appearance with the occupation of the Ionian Islands.

Selim fought luckless wars with both these powers and a host of internal enemies as well. In the wake of Napoleon's disaster in Egypt arose Mehmet Ali, an Albanian adventurer who became modern Egypt's first independent ruler. In Greece, he faced another Albanian adventurer, Ali Tepelenli. In Serbia, the Bosnian *dahijas* who ruled Belgrade cared not a fig for his authority, however solemnly they, and Ali as well, publicly proclaimed it. They knew who the real master of Stamboul was. It was their own Janissary Corps.

Selim's fears were reflected in the memorandum he ordered his principal secretary, Ahmet Atif Efendi, to prepare for the Divan. Its words sounded a tocsin of alarm in no equivocal fashion: "At the time when France was in grave straits and afflicted by dearth and famine," the *reis ül-kütüb* wrote,

27

... the Empire allowed the export of copious supplies from the God-protected realms and their transport to the ports of France, and thus saved them from the pangs of hunger.

In recompense, the French Republic and its generals have not refrained from trying by word and deed to subvert the subjects of the Empire. In particular, at the time of the partition of Venice, they seized the islands and four towns on the mainland near Arta, to wit: Butrinto, Parga, Preveza and Vonitza; *their action in recalling the form of government of the ancient Greeks and installing a regime of liberty in these places reveals beyond any need for comment or explanation the evil intentions in their minds.*[44]

The equation of constitutional liberty with the ancient glories of Hellas, however attenuated the concept in the popular mind, gained acceptance among Greek intellectuals. The "underground best seller" among them was the "Hellenic Nomarchy" which expounded this principle.

Some said the "Hellenic Nomarchy"—anonymously printed outside the sultan's domains—was the work of Rhigas Pheraios. Others attributed the authorship to his disciple, Perrhaebus.[45] Still others saw the author as one Dr. John Kolettes who outwardly appeared most devoted to Ali Pasha but who would someday become prime minister of a free Greece.

More than a century and a half later, the real authorship of the book continues to intrigue Greek historians. But the influence it had upon literate Greeks in its time, combined with the broadsides of Rhigas' revolutionary verse printed and circulated throughout Greece through the zeal of Perrhaebus and Father Hydromenos, was incalculable. And, in France itself, the Chian professor Adamantios Koraes of the University of Montpelier was issuing annotated editions of the ancients and writing essays to inspire the Greek awakening. Among his correspondents was an American classicist and the soul of the American Revolution—Thomas Jefferson.

Epirotes who travelled abroad to Corfu and Venice, or farther afield to Vienna, Marseilles, Paris, the Danubian Principalities and St. Petersburg brought back goods—and ideas—to the seething satrapy of Ali Pasha.

To combat the empire's internal and external dangers, Sultan Selim advocated increased centralization. This meant an end to insubordinate provincial warlords, a modern army and the eventual disbanding of the Janissary Corps. The immediate fruits of this policy were the rebellion of Pasvan Oglu Pasha of Vidin and the revolt of the *dahijas* of Belgrade. Although the pasha of Vidin was crushed, the *dahijas* proved troublesome.

[44] Ahmet (Pasa) Cevdet, *Vekayiyi Devleti Aliye*, Vol. VI, p. 311 et seq., 2nd ed., (in Turkish), Istanbul, 1877 (1294 A.H.), my italics.

[45] Perrhaebus wrote a remarkable *History of Souli and Parga*. See N. Bees, *The Extant works of Perrhaebus*, Athens 1956.

The ensuing melee gave the Christian Serbs the welcome opportunity, under Karageorge and then Milos Obrenovic, to shake both their native feudal masters and the sultan from their backs. What thus began as a struggle between the sultan and his local Moslem satraps ended in the creation of the Christian state that was later to become the nucleus of modern Yugoslavia.

Viewed in the light of subsequent events and the similar form they were to take, the sultan's Serbian disaster was a dress rehearsal for the Greek War of Independence as well. Like the subsequent Greek struggle, the Serbian fight for freedom, begun in 1804, lasted a decade. Again, like the Greek Revolution, the same "Ottoman fire brigade" against the blaze of freedom was called out. The Ghegs of Dibra, Mati and Shkodra, later to measure their fire with the defenders of Missolonghi and the Acropolis, marched into Serbia.

The Serbian ballad of the battle of Deligrad tells us that, when the Serbian uprising occurred,

> Then Bushatli Vezir raised his forces,
> Men from fierce Malesija he gathered,
> And from Skadar on Bojana river,
> Men he gathered from the plains of Mirdit
> All the fearsome Latins from the seaboard,
> And Gjon Marko's son he set before them.[46]

Ali Pasha's Lab scavengers were also called upon to fight, but Ali led them only as far as Macedonia where they sacked Naousa and Monastir and retired with their booty to Yannina.[47] The sultan's failure in subordinating the provincial satraps who were in league with the Janissaries had served to alert the aghas of the corps in Constantinople to his design, but he stubbornly—and fatally—persisted in his plan. A French military manual which had been translated into Arabic for Mehmet Ali's use in Egypt was the basis for the first modern Turkish manual which Selim had translated. Then Selim began the training of a new unit—his *Nizam Cedit* which was to serve as cadre for a modern army.

When he announced that this unit would have its first public drill in Constantinople, the Janissary aghas ordered the corps' soup kettles overturned—the corps' traditional warning that the sultan's head was in jeopardy. In a drama that lasted 90 days, the Janissaries pulled a palace coup, had Selim murdered and replaced him with their creature, Sultan Mustafa.

[46] W. A. Morison, Ph.D., (tr.), *Revolt of the Serbs Against the Turks (1804-1813); Translations from the Serbian National Ballads of the Period,* Cambridge, England 1942, p. 96.

[47] The ballad of the sacking of Naousa is to be found in Panagiotes Aravantinos, *Chronography of Epirus,* 2 vols., Athens 1856, Vol. II, p. 116.

The governor of Rustchuk, Mustafa Bayraktar, was loyal to his master —a quality that did not particularly distinguish the Ottoman pashas of those times. He sped to Constantinople, stormed the palace and entered to free Selim. But Selim was dead, and his cousin Mahmoud, sought by Mustafa's executioners, had been spirited to the safety of a disused stove in the palace *hamam* (bathhouse). When Mustafa was disposed of, Mahmoud, still sooty, emerged to greet his liberators and gird the sword of Osman.

The year in which these events took place was 1808. It would take Mahmoud 18 years to get rid of the Janissaries. While it was not immediately apparent, Mahmoud meant to be his own master and he meant to conclude the work begun by Selim.

More despotic, but less precipitous than Selim, Mahmoud II made Mustafa Bayraktar his grand vizier and cautiously plotted his next moves, one of which was the downgrading and eventual removal of Ali Pasha Tepelenli. Selim had attempted to discipline Ali with half-measures that backfired, as had all his other plans and projects. After Ali's sack of Naousa and Monastir during the Serbian campaign, the sultan stripped him of his title of Vali of Roumelia. In 1805, he was replaced as pasha of Trikkala by Elmaz Bey, Shahinica's son. Elmaz, however, was carried off by a smallpox epidemic and his Constantinopolitan connections soon obtained Ali's reappointment to the post.

The next year, Ali laid hands on the feudal estates of the beys of Thesprotia on the pretext that they were plotting against him. The accused leader of the beys, Hasan Çapari, was brought to Yannina and imprisoned in the fortress tower. There he remained until some 15 years later when, during the Ottoman siege, Çapari's would-be liberators bombarded the fortress. A chance mortar shell hit the tower and Çapari was killed. Çapari's sons, however, fled to the protection of Mehmet Ali of Egypt and were joined there by other Thesprotian beys—Islam Pronjo, Maliq Grava, Jusuf Demo, Xhemo Bazina and Malo Hyso. But, despite the plots hatched in Cairo and Constantinople, Ali grew more powerful than ever. The Sanjaks of Delvino and Berati were subdued and occupied and, as in Trikkala and Yannina, huge feudal estates were seized by Ali and converted into his personal property.[48]

In 1812, Mahmoud transferred Veli Pasha from his Peloponnesian pashalik on the alleged complaint of the beys and aghas of Tripolitsa. Veli was thereupon given Ali's old pashalik in Thessaly and Muhtar, who had been governing Trikkala for his father, was sent to govern Berati. Salih Bey, Ali's youngest son, was named pasha of Lepanto. Accompany-

---

[48] A list of Ali's feudal holdings shortly before his deposition is given in Aravantino's *History of Ali Pasha Tepelenli*, pp. 601-611. The Greek ballad relating to the capture of Berati will be found in Fauriel, op. cit., p. 200.

ing Veli from Tripolitsa to his new pashalik was a man Ali, who had spies everywhere, known to be in league with the beys who had fled to Egypt and who was attempting to turn Veli against his father. This man, Ismail Pasha Bey, was serving as Veli's secretary and Ali, determined to do him in, dispatched a goon squad of seven of his bodyguards to do the job. The seven waylayed Ismail, but he succeeded in killing four and capturing two. One alone escaped to face the Lion's rage. Ismail did not tarry, but fled to the protection of Beqir Pasha of Euboia and thence directly to the sultan himself where he served as Mahmoud's direct link with the exiled beys and aghas Ali had dispossessed.

Through the sullen Janissaries and his own agents, Ali was fully aware of the net that had been spread for him, but he held back from open rebellion, knowing perhaps that, for all his seeming power, he had thousands who would clamor for his head. Mahmoud's plan was in its final stage by 1818, but it was not until October 1819, while Veli was in Yannina attending his son Mehmet's wedding, that the first blow fell. Veli was stripped of his pashalik and named to the "flea-bitten" pashalik of Lepanto. As a consolation, Salih whom Veli displaced was sent by Ali to govern Elbasan and Ochrida. In Veli's place, Mahmoud named a loyal Bosnian, Süleyman Pasha.

Ali, who had not expected such decisive swiftness from Mahmoud, was thunderstruck, although the motive for the move could have been no mystery to him. A family conference was called by Ali in Preveza in January 1820. On the agenda were two questions. The first was whether or not to defy the sultan. The second, just as thorny, was whether to smash the Greek conspiracy of the Friendly Society whose existence right under Ali's nose had been revealed to him by an informer a short time before. If he was to fight the sultan, Ali reasoned, he could use all the aid he could get.

Ali's line of reasoning here is clear. If he succeeded, he could smash the conspiracy of the Greeks at his leisure. With the aid of a Janissary insurrection in Constantinople, he could even dictate his own terms to a cowed sultan. If he failed, nothing would matter. Ali knew, too, that arms were being smuggled by the Greeks and were being surreptitiously distributed to the rayas throughout his domains through the diligent efforts of Perrhaebus and John Paparrhegopoulos, the Russian consul in Patras. Deciding to stall for time to prepare his defense, Ali entered into correspondence with Paparrhegopoulos and called the Greek notables to inform them that all their secrets were known to him. He told them his information was sufficiently thorough to destroy every member of the secret society in continental Greece, but that he would forgive and forget if they supported him against the sultan. He even spoke of a constitution guaranteeing their rights.

In turn, the Greeks knew only too well that their master was clutching at straws. They decided, however, to play along with him so that, in a struggle pitting Ali against the sultan, both could be weakened sufficiently to allow a general Greek uprising this time to succeed.

On Feb. 27, 1820, the sultan struck a second blow. He stripped Ali of his command of the passes and bestowed the title of *dervedat nazir*— and the power that went with it—on the new pasha of Trikkala. At the same time, Veli was stripped of his last and most insignificant pashalik of Lepanto. Veli withdrew, but left a garrison of his own men inside, to the chagrin of his successor. Ali's agents brought him word that his own removal—and Ismail Pasho Bey's appointment in his place—would be Mahmoud's third and final blow from which there would be no redress. Ali decided on a counterstroke. On March 2, within the "sanctified precincts" of the Topkapu Palace itself, Ali's assassins fired upon Ismail, but the shots went wild and Ali, on March 9, was told of the failure.

On March 16, the treasonable dealings of his agent Elmaz Meço Bono with the Janissaries were exposed and Ali's men were ordered expelled from Constantinople. Yet the sultan did not immediately declare Ali an outlaw, but continued the process of amputation. By imperial decree, the Sanjaks of Elbasan and Ochrida Ali had occupied were ordered turned over to the pasha of Shkodra. Nureddin Pasha was appointed governor of Berati and Valona.

This time, the sultan's knife had reached the bone and Ali would yield no more, but ordered his fortifications and troops to be ready for war. In May, he called his lieutenants together to receive their oath, readily given, that they would give him their absolute loyalty. It needed only the approach of the enemy, however, for each of them to name his price for defection.

Finally, in July, the long anticipated imperial decree was issued. It was accompanied by the *fetva* of the sheikh ul-Islam, the supreme kadi Haci Halil Efendi, declaring Ali an apostate against whom it was lawful for Moslems to war. Ismail Pasha, as expected, was named Ali's successor and was appointed *serasker* or commander-in-chief of the forces to be fielded against him. These forces—initially the combined armies of Mahmoud Dramali Pasha of Thrace and Hasan Baba Pasha of Salonica—were joined by the hordes of Mustafa Bushatli Pasha of Shkodra, the Vali of Roumelia Mehmet Pasha of Monastir and other lesser Ottoman luminaries.

Ismail Pasha Plasa took Berati without battle and Ali's sons, Muhtar and Salih, fled to Argyrocastron and afterwards surrendered, as did Veli and his sons Mehmet and Selim. A small Turkish fleet fitted out in the Peloponnese landed Ali's old foe, Shahin Meto Bey Delvina's men at Panormos (Porto Palermo), Santi Quaranta and Buthrotum (Butrinto). These occupied Delvino, St. Basil and Ali's fortresses at Mouzina Pass.

Travelling southwest by way of Grevena and Elassona, Ismail Pasha's troops reached Metsovo at the crossroads of the Pindus Epirus-Thessaly route on Aug. 15 and then descended to the plain of Yannina. Ymer Bey Vrioni put up a feeble resistance, swung over to Ismail's side and was made a pasha. Ali's other lieutenants—Selihtar (Zylyftar) Poda, Dervish Hasan and Ago Vasiari—one by one brought their contingents among Ali's 32,000 men over to the side of the 80,000 besiegers.

Yannina, repeatedly put to the torch by both sides and sacked from end to end, lay in shambles about the invaders who now pounded at Yannina's citadel. Ali barricaded himself within Litharitsa, a fortress-palace he had built within the citadel in 1807 at the southeastern end. Failing to take it, Ismail Pasha was relieved and the capable Mora Valesi Khurshid (Reshid) Pasha was named his successor in March 1821. It was not until November of that year that the Gheg defenders of Litharitsa under Hariz Gjaska were bought off by Khurshid and opened the gates to the besiegers.[49]

On the night of Jan. 9, 1822, by arrangement, Khurshid Pasha allowed the citadel to be evacuated. The cited eyewitness writes that all who wished to leave were rowed across to Perama with their possessions. Among those who left were Ali's cannoneers together with

> . . . Ismail Bey, son of the former Veli Pasha, together with his uncle, Sylejman Pasha, son of Ibrahim Pasha of Berati, and they surrendered and were quartered in the residence of Ymer Pasha Vrioni and thus the citadel was emptied by the 12th. And then they opened the great door and the men of the king stood by and allowed no one to enter because the tower (*iç kale*) is closed and in it is the apostate himself with his treasures and he is guarded by Bajram, Thanasses Vayas, Manthos Dovras, Fehim Çami, Selfo Meço Bono and many others and we do not know what has been spoken of him, whether he would be killed, whether his life would be granted and he would be given a place somewhere to live, or something else we know not what. This alone we see, that as long as he is in the *iç kale,* they do not fire at all on those outside, but allow them to carry themselves out peacefully, why only they know.

Why Khurshid's men did not fire became clear soon enough. Along with his remaining men, his treasures and his Christian wife, Vasilike (nee Contaxes), was the powder magazine of the fortress. One unguarded move by the besiegers, and Ali intended to blow himself up. But this final gesture, so like that contemplated by Hitler in his Berlin bunker, was not to be. Ali let himself be persuaded that he could still bargain for

---

[49] An anonymous but well-informed eye-witness account of the siege from a manuscript in the handwriting of Athanasius Psalidas (1767-1829) and found in the Giannes Vlachogiannes archives was published in its entirety by Neos Koubaras; *Annual of Epirote Chronography,* Vol. II, Athens, 1961. Reprint with introduction and notes by Angelos N. Papakostas, 1962.

his life and his personal property and, on Jan. 20, with 300 men, allowed himself to be taken to the monastery of St. Panteleimon on the island in the center of Yannina's lake, there to await Khurshid's negotiators. We shall see anon what happened there.

It was left to the Moslems of Epirus—Ali's kinsmen, opponents and betrayers—to create the ballad recounting the events of his two-year resistance. It is a curious melange of naivete and bad faith. The inevitable, that the "king and the Lion should quarrel," is presented with amazement. Then we are told that Ali sought an amnesty because he was innocent of injustice and avarice! His troops, accurately enough, are first shown resisting and then abandoning him to his fate. There is only a hint that his resistance had stirred up a force that would long be remembered after Ali was forgotten—the Greek Revolution. He is shown boasting of his will to resist and, in the next breath, to immolate himself, which is the point at which the ballad's narrative breaks off. Yet this is precisely what, in the end did not happen, and Ali did exactly what the anonymous balladeer says he would never do—throw himself upon Khurshid's mercy. There is no mention whatsoever of Ismail Pasha Bey.

Finally and most curiously, we are told that Ali was betrayed by his kin and his minions and—with apparently no grasp of the contradiction— we are then told that he was not betrayed but destroyed by exterior force.

14.

Ashtu qënkish e thanë
për Vezir Ali Pashanë!

Thus was it fated to be
For Vizier Ali Pasha!

Kujtdo i shkonj nëpër fiqir
nga ay mirt të madh lëbet?
T'a dini me të vërtet
trimërija e tij u dijtë,
pse i tilli vezir më s'mbet
të vij sot në këtë ditë.

Who could even raise a thought
That great terror would overtake him!
Learn then that in truth
He displayed his courage,
For a vizier like unto him
Can come no more in this day.

Ditën e Sulltan Nevruzit
na erdhi i zi haberi:
Mëri e sulltan Mahmutit
u përpiq Ali Eshderi.
Asnjë s'e vin' ndë përmendë
që të prish Mbreti Asllanë.
Që ra ndë mëri të mbretit
ahu gjet Ali Pashanë.

On the Sultan's New Year Day
Came to us the black tidings:
The disfavor of Sultan Mahmoud
Has befallen Ali the Dragon.
No such thing could be imagined
That the king would destroy the Lion.
When he felt the king's displeasure
Uneasiness found Ali Pasha.

Qërthëlluar njëzet muaj,
trazoj detet dhe stëret.
Thotë ay luftë s'duaj,
paq të bëje me dovlet.
I thoni Sulltan Mahmutit
t'i çonj një jitlak fermanë;

For twenty months surrounded,
He stirred up sea and land.
He said the war he willed not;
Peace he would make with the realm.
Let Sultan Mahmoud be told
To send him a writ of amnesty.

kësaj punë i gjëj hudut	Let him end this punishment,
pse prishë tërë dynjanë.	For the whole world is being wrecked.
"U bëj vukuf, Sulltan Mahmut!	"Give credence, Sultan Mahmoud!
Mos u dëgjo Shejislamnë!	Listen not to the *sheikh islam!*
Këtë ditë s'e mendova	I cannot this day remember
t'a qesh lënë ndë Sheriat,	To have lapsed from the Sacred Law,
të shtrëmbrën e tepërova	To have acted crooked and grasping
që kur jesh ndë hyqymat."	When I might have been called to judge."

Ditënë që hyri Gushti,	In the beginning of August
nizami fushat i mbushi.	The army filled the plains.
Kërcit topi e kumbaraja;	The cannon and shot explode;
në Janin' u zu nizaja.	In Yannina the war commences.
Që nga Stamboll në Janinë	From Istanbul to Yannina
shumë asqer po na vinë,	Much soldiery comes toward us,
Rushit Pash' me Dramallinë,	Khurshid Pasha and Dramali,
të lëftojn' me Ali Velinë.	To battle with Ali Veli.
Thanë na vjen Rumelija	They say Roumelia sends us
njëzet e dy pashallarë.	Two and twenty pashas.
Urdhëroftë Perëndia	Let God be praised
e na qitë faqe bardhë!	That we emerge white-faced!

Kush ka parë Asllan Alinë	Who has seen Ali the Lion
nd'atë shkretëne Janinë?	In this barren Yannina?
Ndë kala mbylltur të zinë	Locked in the tower, the blackened one
rreh të kthenjë Shqipërinë.	Plots turn over Albania.
Një mij Gegë e dy mij Toskë	A thousand Ghegs and two thousand Tosks
qendruan me Ali Pashanë.	Gathered with Ali Pasha.
Ata vunë kryet poshtë,	These layed down their heads,
me kordhë në dor' u vranë.	With sword in hand they were slain.
Dërgoj fjalë posht' e lartë,	He sends word low and high,
trazoj kahuristanë.	He agitates the infidel lands.
Tahir Abazi, një plak,	Tahir Abas, an elder,
ndë Suli e ngriti rajanë.	Calls out the rayas in Souli.

Mbë njëzet e një të Gushtit	On the twenty-first of August
ia rrethuan kalanë.	They have encircled his tower.
Topi krisi të Shtunën	The cannon went off on Saturday
prej kalasë anëmbanë.	From the castle top to bottom.
Duro, gjule e kumbara,	Hold shot and shell,
moj kalaja me bedena,	Oh fortified tower,
pse lëfton me padishah	For with the emperor makes war
Ali Pash' Tepelena!	Ali Pasha the Tepelenian!
O, moj ti , kula serhatë	Oh you, extended tower
që mban Matjan e Dibranë,	Where the Matians and Dibrans hold,
trimat me besë që patë	You have honorable warriors,
Mahmut Bejnë me Allemanë!	Mahmoud Bey and Alemani!
Raqip Bej, bëni gajret!	Rakip Bey, have courage!
E ju, asqer i kalasë,	And you, troops of the tower,
pse kemi për dyzet vjet	For we have twenty years worth
zahire kësaj belasë!	Of provisions to stem this trouble!

Të parë shtatë vezirë	The first seven viziers
seç u hodhnë ndë Janinë.	Threw themselves on Yannina.

Hedhin gjule me zinxhirë
sipër mbi Vezir Alinë.
Bijë gjulet treqind okë
mbushur barut edhe gozhdë.
Levendët e Kara Aliut
ç'i rreh top' i Osmanlliut.
Kalaja n'anët gjollit
ç'e rreh topi i Stambollit.
Një kala në anët detit
i dolli karshi dovletit.
Një kala në anët gjollit
i ktheu gjoksin Stambollit!

Qytahiu hipi jedishnjë
që të marrë Lithariçnjë.
Në portë të Lithariçit
kullon gjak pall' e Rushitit.
Shkoj Ali t'u jep gajret,
asqer t'a syll mbë karar.
I gjet ndë mushaveret
kur i bëjnë kokën pazar!
U përpiq, o, i gjori plak!
Ndë xhephane e ke folenë.
Se të digjesh, e ke me hak,
zaptovë tërë dhenë!

Dalldisi pashaj si burrë;
tha: "Që unë? S'bënet kurrë
të Rushiti s'jepëm,
t'a dini, pse unë s'trëmbëm.
Forcat e zëmër s'më mbeti;
ikën Gegët e me lanë.
Më ra përsipër dovleti,
do t'm'e krej binanë.
Po Zoti durim m'i dhashtë,
se unë do të përpiqem
sa të kam gjak edhe eshtrë.
Unë i gjall nuk jepëm.

"Ç'faj u kam të mijvet unë
që m'a bënë këtë dhunë?
Veli Aga Grebeneja
veç m'u ndodh për Këtë punë.
Ç'u bërë, mor' Thanas Vaja?
As u hidh, dil nga kalaja!
Pa pyesni Zharkallinjtë
ku e lan' Ali Pashanë?
Bejller bëra Evgjitë,
po ata jan' soj çobanë.
Dhe ju, Labër, zënë çifuti,
më latë mua fatzinë.
Ju preftë Sulltan Mahmuti
pse prishtë vetën shtëpinë.

They cast shot with chain
Over on Vizier Ali.
Three hundred oka shell is falling
Full of nails and gunpowder.
The braves of Kara Ali
Are sought by the cannon of the Osmanli.
The tower by the edge of the lake
Is singled out by Istanbul's cannon.
A tower by the water's edge
Draws up to withstand the empire.
A tower by the edge of the lake
Has buried itself in Istanbul's breast!

Kütahi mounted his steed
To conquer Litharitsa.
At Litharitsa's gate
Khurshid's sword drips blood.
Ali rises to give them courage,
To range in order his troops.
He finds them in consultation
Offering his head for sale!
Strike, oh luckless man!
You have your nest in the powder store.
Though you would burn up, the cause is
      yours,
You have seized the whole world!

Like a man the pasha resisted;
Said he: "What I? It shall never be
That I surrender to Khurshid,
Know now, for I'm not afraid.
Power and heart hold no longer;
The Ghegs have gone and left me.
Upon me has fallen the empire
Wishing to raze my foundation.
But the Lord give me endurance,
For I will strike back
While I have blood and bone.
I shall not surrender alive.

"What fault have I done to mine own
That they have done this evil to me?
Veli Agha of Grevena
Alone stood by me for this struggle.
Where can you be, oh Thanassi Vaya?
Jump out, come forth from the castle!
Go question the Zarkalis
Where they abandoned Ali Pasha.
Beys I have made of Gypsies,
But these are the kin of shepherds.
And you, Laburia, like a busy Jew
You've left me to my misfortune.
Let Sultan Mahmoud cut you down
For you've destroyed your own house.

"Të mijtë m'a bënë dhunë,
Janinë nizam m'a prunë.
Djemt e mi, si çifuti
që më lanë mua plaknë,
i preftë Sulltan Mahmuti;
më turpuruanë oxhaknë.

"Ku jini ju, parësija?
Pas vdekjes s'ime, ç'do të thoni
kur t'i u shajn' Osmanllia?
Vallahi, ju ç'do të bëni?
Janinë, Janin' e shkretë,
c'të paç ndërtuarë vetë.
S'të gëzova as vet' as djemtë.
Të raftë zjarri të djegtë.
Të djegtë anëmbanë
bashkë me Ali Pashanë!

"E mbë tej, ku do të vemi?
Bëri be Fehim i mirë:
'Vasiliqi, zjarr' e kemi
të digjemi me vezirë.' "

Nd'atë kohë ay po u flit:
"Fehim, të përpiqemi!
Vasiliqi, merr me fitiltë
foga e të digjemi!"

Kështu deshi Perëndia
që u çkulen mbretëria;
vezirit i'u prish kapia.
Njëmij e treqint rixhallinjë
që i mbaj veziri pranë,
me dorë e dhan' të gjallë.

Shtatëdhjet vjet që rrove,
sa zë dielli dhe shtrove.
S'os të dhanë vilaeti,
po të gremisi dovleti.
I Madhi Vezir,
t'erdhi me pa hyr'!

"Mine own have done me an evil deed,
To Yannina they've brought me the army.
My sons, like a Jew
That they've left aged me,
Let Sultan Mahmoud hew them down;
They have disgraced my hearth.

"Where are you, notables?
After my death, what will ye say
When the Osmanlis disgrace you?
By Allah, what will you do?
Yannina, barren Yannina,
With mine own hands I built you.
I did not enjoy you, nor did my children.
Let fire fall and consume you.
May you burn from top to bottom
Together with Ali Pasha!

And afterwards, where shall we go?
The good Fehim has sworn an oath:
'Vasilike, we have fire,
Let us burn up with the vizier.' "

At that moment he called to them:
"Fehim, let us strike!
Vasilike, carry by wick
A flame and let us burn up!"

Thus it was that God had willed
That the kingdom uproot him;
The vizier's tower was destroyed.
A thousand three hundred followers
The vizier held beside him
By their hand gave him up alive.

In the seventy years that you lived,
You subdued as much as the sun shone upon.
You were not betrayed by the province,
But the empire tore you down.
Oh Great Vizier,
It came about 'gainst your will!

The final scene in the life of Ali Pasha was played out on Tuesday, Jan. 24, 1822 in the small, two-story guest house of the monastery on the island, which still stands today.[50] There Ali awaited the emmissaries of Khurshid who were to draw up the terms of his surrender. What followed is described in full by Charles François Pouqueville who had been, for many years, Napoleon's envoy to Ali.[51]

[50] The author visited the site in late August 1962.

[51] Charles François Pouqueville, *Histoire de la Régénération de la Grèce*, vol. III, pp. 374-6, Paris 1824.

It was five o'clock when the vizier, who was sitting opposite to the entrance gate, saw arrive with gloomy countenances, Hasan Pasha, Ymer Vrioni, (Köse) Mehmet, Khurshid's *selihtar,* his *kaftandji,* several officers of the army and a numerous suite.

At their appearance, Ali rose with impetuosity, his hand on the pistols in his girdle.

"Stop! What do you bring me?" he exclaimed to Hasan in a voice of thunder.

"The will of his Highness. Do you know these august characters?"

He showed him the brilliant gilded frontispiece which adorned the firman.

"Yes, I reverence it."

"Well then, submit to fate. Make your ablutions. Address your prayer to God and the Prophet. Your head is demanded by . . ."

"My head," replied Ali, furiously interrupting him, "is not to be given up so easily."

These words were no sooner uttered, then they were followed by a pistol shot, which wounded Hasan in the thigh. With the rapidity of lightning, Ali killed the *kaftandji* and his guards, firing at the same moment on the crowd, brought down several *chohadars.*

The terrified Ottomans fled from the pavilion. Ali perceived that he was bleeding. He was wounded in the breast.

He roared like a bull. They fired from all parts on the kiosk, and four of his *pallikars* fell at his side.

He no longer knew where to make head. He heard the noise of his assailants beneath his feet. They fired through the wooden floor which he trod. He had just received a shot in his side. Another, firing upwards from below, hit him in the spine. He tottered, caught onto a window and fell on a sofa.

"Run," he cried to one of his *chohadars.* "Go, my friend, and dispatch poor Vasilike that the unhappy woman may not be outraged by these wretches."

The door opened. All resistance was at an end. The *pallikars* who ceased to defend the tyrant jumped out the windows. The *selihtar* of Khurshid Pasha entered, followed by the executioners.

Ali was still full of life.

"Let the justice of God be done," said a kadi and, at these words, seizing the criminal by the beard, the executioners dragged him under the peristyle. There, placing his head on a stair, they had to strike repeatedly with a notched cutlass before they could effect his decapitation.

It is said that, when the head was brought to Khurshid, he paid it the honor of receiving it standing. Stuffed with cotton and spices, it was forwarded to Constantinople where, after a display outside the palace gates, it was claimed by a Bektashi monk—Dervish Sylejman—who had it enterred in front of the cemetery near the Selymbrian Gate. At the command of the authorities, the following inscription was caused to be engraved on the headstone:

"There is none who is ignorant of what considerations and how many benefactions Tepelenli Ali Pasha enjoyed for 30 or 40 years beneath the shadow and protection of the Sublime Porte, and how many grants were bestowed by high decree both unto him and unto his sons and all those about him.

"But withal, counting as nothing such benefactions and always showing his formal ingratitude in opposition to the will of the Sublime Porte, his benefactor, i.e., having gathered about him until now unnumbered tokens of its good will, this man left no injustice uncommitted upon its subjects, the servants of God.

"The unlawful acts and unauthorized practices committed by this man have never before been heard of or seen. He was never at rest. Were there anywhere a revolution or rebellion, he was either the apparent or hidden prime mover. He participated in it and supplied it with either money or provisions.

"Not being satisfied with the lands and territories entrusted to his administration, he hastened to extend the bounds of his jurisdiction to other provinces, instigating disorders and upheavals in order to succeed in his purpose.

"He seized the property of some. He trod the honor of others underfoot. He exterminated whole families. He became the scourge of unfortunate subjects who are a pawn of great value entrusted by the Most High to the safekeeping of the one Monarch alone.

"He expunged many families in Albania, in Yenisehr (Larissa), in Monastir, in Sarigol and other places to which he was able to extend his murderous arm, and with such injustices drove many families and numerous inhabitants of those places to despair so that they abandoned their country.

"The Sublime Porte, having knowledge of his coercive acts, advised him many times to change his behavior and to reflect upon his wretched end. Nevertheless, he never desired to reflect upon these, his repeated offenses, but always continued to trod upon his evil path.

"As the climax of his infidelity and evildoing, in order to take revenge upon persons he hated because they were opposed to him and had fled to the Seat of State, Constantinople, he attempted a daring conspiracy against their lives, firing at them two shots by the hands of agents he had delegated for this purpose.

"Then, in order to redress his insults to the majesty of the State, it became necessary to punish him, and he was first relieved of his satrapy and the administration of his provinces was entrusted to another.

"He then, however, declaring himself an apostate and imagining he could succeed in his infidel designs, having long since fortified the Castle of Ioannina, was certain he could resist the might of his great benefactor, the Sublime Porte.

"He revealed thereby the secret conspiracy he had entered into with the rebellious Greeks and he dispatched large sums to the Peloponnese and to the Souliotes, encouraging them to arm themselves against the Moslem folk. By these acts he gave notice that he was neither more nor less than an irreligious and faithless man.

Therefore, because his death was demanded by law and the rights of the State, the Satrap of Roumelia and Commanding General Khur-

shid Pasha captured the evildoer who, in accordance with the legal
decision of the Holy Fetva and in conformity with the terrible decree
of the Well-Governed Realm, had brought upon himself the death
penalty, and thus were the Moslem people liberated from this apostate
subject's coercion and tyranny.

"This is the head of the aforementioned indubitable traitor Tepelenli
Ali Pasha."

"HAIL, OH LIBERTY! HAIL"
(1820-1828)

The Greeks had no time to pause when they learned of the beheading of Ali, for they were preoccupied with another struggle—their own. Kolokotronis, with his accustomed brevity, notes in his memoirs: "The downfall of Ali Pasha helped us much; it was needful that he should be removed, he was a great brute." Makrigiannes, too, wastes no rhetoric in noting Ali's death. "On January 24, 1822," he wrote, "they slew Ali Pasha like an ox, for tyrants are afraid to die like warriors. At his age, he wanted to live on yet to tyrannize."[52]

The Greeks in general rose up against their masters with only the vaguest idea of how they would succeed—and they succeeded. The Friendly Society, on the other hand, as the self-appointed elite of the revolution, had an elaborate and ambitious plan—and failed. The plan was set into motion on Feb. 23, 1821, by the Greek ruler of what is now Rumania, Prince Alexander Hypsilanti, who had been designated commander-in-chief by the Society. The Hetairist plan was to secure the Danubian Principalities while Ali's death throes diverted the main body of the Ottoman armies elsewhere. Success in expelling the Turks from Moldavia and Wallachia would encourage the autonomous Serbs to proclaim their full independence and complete the liberation of all the Serbian provinces. Perhaps the Bulgars, then stolidly enduring the Turkish yoke, would also rise and Orthodox Russia could be embroiled. A federation of Balkan Christian states with a Romanov ruling Constantinople would insure the end of Ottoman tyranny forever.

There were several things wrong with this theoretically impressive scheme. In the first place, the Greeks in Rumania were a foreign ruling class which could command little sympathy, let alone sacrifice, from the Rumanian peasantry. Secondly, the pro-Russian Karageorge was no longer the ruler of Serbia and the Obrenovic monarch was quite comfortable with the arrangements made with the Turks. Third, the Russian Tsar was busily proclaiming to his fellow monarchs the principle of the

---

[52] General John Makrigiannes, *Memoirs* (Vlachogiannes, ed.) Athens, 1947, p. 22.

41

legitimacy of Divine Right embodied in a Holy Alliance against freedom anywhere. And, even if the Tsar should have thought otherwise, there were the British and their fleet to be reckoned with and the British never had any stomach for Russian aspirations toward Constantinople.

On June 7, 1821, with his aide de camp Athanasius Pipes of Vouno and his Chimarriote braves at his side, Hypsilanti drew up to face the enemy in the engagement which was to determine the Rumanian campaign. The place was Dragatsani in Wallachia. A premature charge by a body of Greek cavalry and the defection of the key Rumanian ally and his troops determined the outcome.[53]

That fateful day and the brave Chimarriotes who fell for the freedom of Greece in far-off Rumania are remembered by the albanophone Epirotes in the following song:

15.

Tetëqint e njëzet viti,	In the year of 1820,
pushka e parë seç krisi.	The first gun was fired.
Lëfton Ipsillant Politi,	Hypsilanti the Politan fights,
i rri pranë Thanas Pipi.	By his side sits Thanasses Pipes.
As i biri Turk jezitit!	Strike the Turkish traitor down!
Në Dunë të gjithë i mbiti.	He drowned them all in the Danube.
Në qafë të Dragocanit	On the ridge of Dragatsani
u vra llohu i Ipsillantit.	Was slain the legion of Hypsilanti.

Back in Greece, the return of the Souliotes from Corfu led to a timely reconciliation of the factions led by the Botsaris and Tzavellas clans and the reoccupation of Souli. Bickering among the Souliotes was not to break out again until the siege of Missolonghi but, for the time being, common cause was made against a common foe. In the hard fighting that followed, George Botsaris' grandson, for all that he had been brought up in the court of Ali Pasha, proved himself the bravest and most devoted of all that fiery breed. When the exiled Souliotes landed, Marcos Botsaris was making preparations for celebrating a new year. It was, indeed, a new year that was to dawn for him and for all Greeks alike.

16.

U nise për Shën Vasi,	For Saint Basil you set forth,
lule moj, Marko Boçari,	Oh blossom Marcos Botsaris,
të bëjë vitin e ri.	To make a New Year.
T'erdhi një haber i ri:	A new notice came to you:
"Marko, ktheu përsëri	"Marco, turn back again
se të kan' zënë pusi.	Because they've staged you an ambush.
Kemi luftë me Turqi!"	We are at war with Turkey!"

[53] *AC,* pp. 43, 44.

In the many battles, both on their home ground and later, farther south, the Souliotes added new laurels to their fame. In 1822, after throwing some of his best troops against the Souliotes at Avarikos, Choni and the fortress of Kiapha, Khurshid ruefully had to admit, as had Ali before him, that "I never imagined, with such numerous and brave Turko-Albanian troops, that I would not defeat today a mere 2,000 Souliotes. I cannot but credit this either to their bravery or to your cowardice and worthlessness which proved them victors."[54]

And everywhere in Greece, when the deeds of the revolutionary commanders were recounted, the name of Botsaris was spoken with awe. Not without a certain respect, but with a deadly hate too, the Moslems, whose descendents sometimes claim him today as an Albanian, created this song:

17.

O, Janinë, pse ke zi?	Oh Yannina, why do you mourn?
Ku je, o, Vezir Ali?	Where are you, Vizier Ali?
Pa del në divan e rri.	Come out to the divan and sit.
Vure qalin në sy.	Put your spyglass to your eye.
Shko një sefer të ri	Behold a new expedition
që të prish mendë tani.	That stuns you out of your mind.
Mos ungjall i vdekuri?	Perhaps the dead have come to life?
Trimat që rritë ty,	The warriors you brought up,
veshur si arrëxhi,	Dressed like vagabonds,
vunë festën mbi sy.	Have donned their fezzes above their eyes.
O, e gjora Vasiliqi,	Oh barren Vasilike,
bënë be në Perëndi,	They have made an oath to God,
ndë kryq që beson dhe ty,	To the cross in which you, too, believe,
(që s'bëhet fjala dy),	(In a word that cannot be twain),
të hidhen mbi Turqi.	To throw themselves upon Turkey.
Andruci në Livadhi	Androutsos in Livadia
dukë thirre "Lefteri!"	Is shouting "Liberty!"
Vuri zjarrë ndë për xhami;	He has set fire to the mosques;
piu gjak Turku e dot s'u fri.	He drinks Turkish blood and is unsated.
Pa kujtohu, o, plak Ali,	Do you recall, Old Man Ali,
një djalë, një çilimi	One boy, one infant
qysh e keshe në avlli?	Whom you had at court?
Një shejtan, një qën i zi,	A devil, a black dog,
ndë nam të shkoj dhe ti.	He has surpassed you in fame.
Dolli gjarpër me mëri.	He turned out a hateful serpent.
Preu dyzet kollëxhi.	He cut down forty officers.
Ky qe Marko Boçari!	This was Marcos Botsaris!
Nëm-past! Si arri,	Damn him! Like a lion
hidhet përmbi ordhi.	He throws himself on the horde.

[54] Perrhaebus, *Complete Works*, p. 126.

A serious attempt by the Greek forces to gain a firm hold on Epirus was precluded by the presence there of the bulk of the Ottoman armies, drawn thither by the duel with Ali. With a general uprising headed by a provisional native administration out of the question, any resistance was ultimately in vain. Yet, again isolated, the magnificent Souliotes were the Greek Revolution in Epirus.

Despite their successful reoccupation and defense of their home territory, their plight resembled that of the final phases of their siege by Ali with one difference—they were not alone. The cause of Souli was shared by the whole Greek nation in arms and demands were made of the revolutionary leadership to aid them. This popular pressure forced Alexander Mavrocordatos, an able politician but a thorough ignoramus in military affairs, to resign his presidency of the provisional Executive Council in southern Greece and to lead an expedition north. Alongside the Greeks in this ill-fated attempt were philhellene volunteers who embraced the struggle of Greece for the same reason their countrymen had embraced earlier the cause of the American Colonies.

If the cause of Souli was the cause of Greece, the Greek cause was nothing less than the cause of liberty. Mirzewski the Pole who had fought with Bolivar, Chevalier the Swiss, Dannia the Italo-Frenchman and General Normann Ehrenfels of Wurtemberg were among the volunteers who followed Mavrocordatos northward despite their misgivings over the military soundness of the venture. Some provisions and arms got through to the Souliotes via the tiny fishing port of Phanari not far from Souli, but the main force sent to Souli's aid set forth overland from the port of Missolonghi on June 1, 1822.

Located on an inlet of the Gulf of Corinth, Missolonghi was an impediment both to the east-west movement of enemy troops and to armies proceeding overland from the northwest to the Peloponnese. It was from this position that Mavrocordato's men moved toward Arta. A Souliote detachment proceeded from Souli to Pente Pigadia ("Five Wells") to effect a juncture. But this latter position, once taken, could not be held, and Mavrocordatos and the Souliotes fell back on Peta without battle. At Peta, however, a disasterous encounter all but wiped them out. The only thing that prevented their total annihilation was the inability of the enemy to move up reinforcements which had been diverted to the siege of Souli.

Marcos Botsaris, who had led the Souliote contingent to the juncture with Mavrocordatos, together with the other survivors of Peta, took refuge at Missolonghi. There they were joined later by the main body of Souliotes who, seeing resistance at Souli at an end, accepted enemy terms to allow their evacuation again to Corfu. From the island they came to Missolonghi to continue their fight. Thus, by late fall 1822, Greeks and philhellenes, military chieftains and politicians, had all gathered at Missolonghi with their backs to the sea, awaiting the inevitable attack by land forces no longer occupied with the suppression of Ali. The revolutionary fleet, albanophone Hydra's merchantmen mounted with cannon, broke the blockade of Missolonghi by Ottoman warships and its defenders were now prepared to hold out indefinitely against the forces of Kütahi and Ymer Pasha Vrioni. On Christmas Eve, thinking the Christians in church, an advance force of Ymer Pasha's Albanians attacked the walls. Hearing no sound, they came in the darkness within pistol range when, to their astonishment, a blast of concentrated fire from the battlements sent them back reeling.

18.

Në Mesollongjin të shkret'
mbrethuar me kënet,
seç filloj luftën me mbret;
lëfton Ismajl Beu vet
me tre mij' e pesëdhjet.
Po lëfton Boçari vet
me shoqëria shtatëdhjet,
të gjitha trima me flet.

In barren Missolonghi
Girded round by marshes,
The war with the king begins;
Ismail Bey himself gives battle
With three hundred and fifty men.
But Botsaris himself gives battle
With seventy companions,
All braves with pleated kilts.

Vat', Ismajl Beu, vatël
U përgjuan palla xhellatë.

Go, Ismail Bey, go!
The headsman's sword was impatiently waited.

Mbetnë taboret në dapje,

The garrison had remained at the battlements,

ato dapje plot pëllëmba
që lëftojn' e s'tundet këmba.

Those battlements full of doves
Who fought and their feet touched no ground.

Ç'kishin pjellur ato nëna?
Kishin pjell e bërë drëna
që lëftojn' me të vërtet
për liri e për të drejt!

To what had those mothers given birth?
They had given birth to deer
Who fought in truth
For freedom and for justice!

The Albanians never recovered from this blow. A few days later, in worse condition than the besieged, they withdrew to Vrachori, leaving behind their cannon and supplies. Fording the Acheloos river, which was swollen by winter snows, 500 were drowned. The rest reached Karvasaras and then Preveza in disorder. But, in time, the Albanians would be back to match their brawn with Missolonghi's defenders. This time they meant to come in such force that their revenge on the hated Greeks would be complete.

On August 5, 1823, an advance force of Mahmoud Pasha of Shkodra, 5,000 men under Xhellaleddin Bey Mirjalli, occupied outposts at Kephalovrysi just outside of Karpenisi where they were joined by the main force of 16,000 men. Upon meeting, the leaders drew up confident plans to advance upon Missolonghi and crush the Souliotes and their fellow infidels.

19.

Bie borë e bie shi;	It snows and it rains;
u nxi jeta, shum' u nxi.	The world is darkened, darkened much.
Ngrijnë krye në Greqi;	They've lifted their head in Greece;
zjarr ndë shumë xhami.	Set fire to many mosques.
Ferman ndë gjithë Turqi:	An order to the whole of Turkey:
"Tundu, o, Mehmet Ali!	"Move, oh Mehmet Ali!
Mbloje detinë gjemi!	Fill the sea with ships!
Zërë qafirë si mi!	Seize the infidels like rats!
Lësho harapin i zi	Let the black Arabs go
të vejë ngjer në Frëngji!	To reach to the Frankish lands!
"Prit' e pritë, o, Rumeli,	"Await, await oh Roumelia,
nizam lloji lloji,	An Army of every sort,
Halldup, Gegë e Toskëri,	Anatolian, Gheg and Tosk,
Shkodranë Pasha të vjen mbi.	Shkodra's pasha to descend upon you.
Dile të shohçe Shkodran Pashanë	Come out and see the Shkodran pasha
me njëzet mijë asllanë!"	With twenty thousand lions!"
Ndë Karpenesh vu bajraknë,	At Karpenisi he plants the standards,
karaul mbë çdo anë.	A lookout at every post.
Pashaj me Mirjallajnë	The pasha and Mirjalli
ndë çadëre mbrënda vanë.	Entered inside the tents.
U mblodhnë bëjnë divanë.	They gathered to hold consultation.
"Inshallah!" të gjithë thanë,	"God willing," they all exclaimed,
"për ndë Mesollongji e kanë.	"They will head toward Missolonghi.
Forra palla e jataganë	Advance the sabres and the scimitars
të nderojnë sulltanë	To honor the sultan
e të shkelin rajanë!"	And to trod down the raya!"
Mesollongji e dëgjon;	Missolonghi heard of it;
vuri vajët e vajton.	It raises a dirge and laments.
Duaj ndihme e ndihme s'gjënë.	It sought aid, but finds it not.
Kapetanët kërkon.	It seeks its captains.
Zuri renkën e rëkon;	It began to heave and sigh
Shqipëtaret veshtron.	Beholding the Albanians.
Ishin brënda Sulote,	Within were the Souliotes,
shahina trima pa anë.	Incomparable warrior falcons.
Nga Suli u ngrenë e vanë	From Souli they had risen and gone
me dyfek e jataganë.	With muskets and with scimitars.

Within Missolonghi, as before in the fight with Ali, the clans of Botsaris and Tzavellas vied for leadership. But Marcos, who had just been invested formally with the command of the Souliotes, silenced his opponents with a gesture. Tearing up his general's commission, he told Kitsos Tzavellas to his face: "Look at the commission that annoys you. Who is bravest will now be shown facing the Shkodran."

And the Shkodran was not long in coming. Refugees from the villages about Karpenisi reached Missolonghi to tell of the powerful force on its way.[55] Botsaris, devising a plan to demoralize the enemy, chose the flower of his meager Souliotes headed by Tousas Zervas and led them where the enemy least expected them—to the Albanian encampment. The chief element of his plan was surprise. The one factor that made it possible was that Botsaris and his brave Greeks spoke the same language as the enemy.

What followed has been celebrated by the Greeks of Northern Epirus in a *Botsariad* which differs in no wise from the story as familiar to every Greek schoolboy as Paul Revere's ride and the execution of Nathan Hale are to young Americans.[56] In this instance, as in every other, this people still under the yoke of their ancient enemy, have rejoiced with their fellow Greeks in their good fortune and cried with them in their sorrow:

20.

Sulltani dërgoj një kartë
të ngrihen gjithë Shkodranët,
Mirditët edhe Matjanët,
Dibranët e Shkupjanët.
Edhe pashaj e këndoj,
Shqipërisë ia dëftoj.

The sultan sent a letter
To arouse all the Shkodrans,
The Mirdites and the Matians,
The Dibrians and the Skopljans.
The pasha had it read,
To Albania he displayed it.

U betuan ndë besë
që të hidhen Morese.
Për një ditë e për një natë
u ngrenë gjithë kazatë.
U hodhnë ndë rrap i gjatë.
Numuroj Shqipërinë;
ndë mëngjez vanë Janinë.
"More trima, të vështojmë

They swore upon their faith
To throw themselves upon Greece.
In a single day and night
All the districts were aroused.
They gathered at the tall plane tree.
The Albanians were counted;
At dawn they reached Yannina.
"Oh braves, let us gaze upon

---

[55] See Demetrius Petropoulos, (ed.), *Greek Folksongs,* (2 vols.), Vol. I, p. 215, Athens, 1959.

[56] Among currently available collections of folksongs in Greek which include ballads recounting this episode, see *ibid.,* p. 216; Agis Theros, (ed.), *Songs of the Greeks,* (2 Vols.), Vol II, p. 60, Athens 1951; Georgia Tarsoule, *Morean Songs of Corone and Methone,* p. 53, Athens 1944; Athanasius Giankas, (ed.), *Epirote Folksongs, 1000-1958,* pp. 161-162, Athens, 1959. Formal poets, too, have vied in eulogizing Botsaris and recounting the episode. One of the earliest elegies, unfortunately only a fragment, will be found in the verse of the author of the Greek national anthem, Dionysios Solomos (1798-1857) for which see his *Complete Extant Works,* Athens, 1965, pp. 203-204. An eye-witness, a lad from the Vlach-speaking Epirote village of Syrraco who was to become one of 19th Century Greece's most distinguished poets, George Zalocostas (1805-1858), chose the episode for what many consider his finest poem, for which see *Works* (Beneficial Books Society edition, Sideres, pub.), pp. 145-223. In the young United States, where its own fight for freedom was still a living memory, Botsaris' heroic death at the age of 33 brought a tear to many an American eye. An American elegy to Greece's immortal freedom fighter was the often-recited poem by Fitz-Greene Halleck (1790-1867), first published in the *New York Review* of June 1825. See Appendix B.

udhën që do të shkojmë,"
u përgjigjë Kapetan Lleshi;
"të shkojmë nga Karpeneshi."

The road we are to travel,"
Remarked Captain Lleshi,
"Let us set forth from Karpenisi."

Kur u hodhnë ndë Komboti,
dëgjoj Marko Suloti.
Digjuan Moraitë,
shkret i lanë shtëpitë.
Erdhën Markos e i thanë:
"Njëzet mijë gjithë janë."

When they gathered at Kompoti,
Marcos the Souliote heard of it.
The Greeks heard of it,
They left their homes abandoned.
They came to Marcos and told him:
"They total twenty thousand."

Ish një burrë, trim i ri,
i zeshkë, mustaq e zi,
po rri me malenkoni.
Mbaj dorën mbi harbi.
Mbaj vesh, s'flit me njeri.
Marko Boçari qe ky!
Mbaj vesh edhe dëgjoj,
psherëtiu edhe rënkoj.

He was a man, a young warrior,
Dark of skin, with black moustache,
But he sat with melancholy mien.
He rested his hand on a ramrod.
He inclined his ear, spoke with no one.
This was Marcos Botsaris!
He inclined his ear and listened,
Snorted and heaved a sigh.

E thirri Tush Bajraktarë
që e kish n'asqer të parë.
E thirri Tushën mbë nj'anë:
"Trimat tanë sa janë?"
"Treqind vetë, kapetanë."
Shoqtë e tij i numuroj,
treqind vetë plot i mbloj.
Nga trimat e tij vështroj,
rrëmbeu karafil' e shkoj.

He called to Tousas the Standardbearer
Who was of the choicest troop.
He called Tousas aside:
"Your braves, how many are they?"
"Three hundred only, captain."
He counted his companions.
Three hundred strong alone he chose.
From his warriors he looked,
Seized his musket and arose.

Tha: "Ndo të vdes, ndo të rroj.
Këtë jetën s'munt t'a shkoj,
nat' e ditë oj e oj."
U thot: "O, shoq! O, asllanë!
Mos e gëzofshi dynjanë
si raja ndë turkallarë.
Vërtet, nuk jemi shumë,
po do të bëjëm një punë
se janë çadëre shumë.
Sonte do t'u derdhim gjaknë,
t'u ndërrojmë din e imanë.
Sonte t'u biem pranë
se kam 'tan a epi tanë'
t'a zë prej mekre pashanë!

Says he: "I shall either live or die.
This life I can bear no longer,
Lamentations night and day."
Said he to them: "Oh comrades, oh lions!
Let this world give you no joy
As rayas of the Turks.
T'is true that many we are not,
But we shall work a scheme
Because the tents are many.
Tonight we shall spill their blood,
We shall overturn their faith.
Tonight we shall fall beside them
For it's my "with it or upon it"
To seize the pasha by the beard!"

"Ju të hidhij anëmbanë,
se u do të vras pashanë,
të bir edhe qehajanë,
të dëgjonj edhe sulltani
ç'është Marko Kapetani,
Marko Boçari Suloti,
Dhrakua e Lepenjoti!

"Throw yourselves hither and yon,
For I shall slay the pasha,
His son and his lieutenant
So the sultan, too, may learn
What this Captain Marcos is,
Marcos Botsaris the Souliote,
Dracos and Lepeniotis!"

"Kadiller e agallarë
t'i pritni me jataganë.
Asnjë mos liri të gjallë.
Të shkuletë kjo farë,
se na poqi, na vu zjarrë
Muhameti me Kuranë.

"Folni Shqip me Shqipëtarë
pra! Flas u me Shkodranë.
'Bam' mos bëni as mbë nj'anë.
Gjashtëdhjet eni pranë
sa të rrëmbej pashanë.
Kadale, o, kordhëtarë,
vrini karaul e parë.
Vrini një, vrini dy,
vrini sa shihni me sy
po si ulqet mbi dhi!"

Allah, Allah, o, Turqi,
atë natë ç'hoqe ti?
Atë natë n'errësi
shkretove kaq ordhi!
Brënda në ordhi që hynë,
vranë gjithë Shqipërinë.
E u ngrenë ndë për gjumë
Turqit që qenë shumë.
Po qysh t'u bëhet halli?
Lëfton "palla e stërralli."
Pa goditëshin në kokë
s'dijnë cijtë janë shokë.

O, shok, me det-medet,
shkoj Markua si mbret.
Pashanë kërkon e s'flet.
Ndë çadëre nuk e gjet.
Zu prej mjekre një lanet,
duke hequr thërret:
"Aman! Thuam, kush je?"
"Un jam, derr, nuk më njeh?"
"Aman! More, cili je ti?"
"Derr i derrit, nuk e di?
Jam një kapetan i ri.
Quhem Marko Boçari.
Arçë vetëm për ti!"

Derr' Turknë e zuri drithmë;
sokëllit vu një thirrmë:
"O, Turqi, në besoni dinë,
të më shpëtoni fatzinë
se kahurët me mbytnë!
Thirri pashaj tashtinë:
"Ku është harapi ynë?"

The kadis and the aghas
Hew down with scimitars.
Not one let free to live.
Let this tribe be uprooted,
For they have roasted us, set us ablaze
By Mohammed and the Koran.

"Call in Albanian to the Albanians
Then! I shall speak to the Shkodran.
Let no one go 'boom' from anywhere.
Let sixty men go with me
Until I seize the pasha.
Slowly, oh swordsmen,
Slay the first outpost.
Slay one, slay two,
Slay whom your eyes behold
But like wolves upon the fold."

Allah, Allah, oh Turkey,
What befell you on that night?
In the darkness of that night
Was wasted such a horde.
When they entered the horde in front,
They slew all the Albanians.
And from slumber they raised up
The Turks who were many.
But how was their destruction wrought?
"Sabre and flint" fought.
Unless struck upon the head
They knew not who was a comrade.

What ho, oh comrades,
Marcos passed through like a king.
He sought the pasha and did not speak.
He found him not within the tent.
By the beard he seized a demon,
Who being dragged yelled:
"Mercy! Tell me, who are you?"
"It is I, swine, don't you know me?"
"Mercy! Hey, tell me who are you?
"Pig of pigs, know you not me?
I am the young captain.
I'm called Marcos Botsaris.
I have come alone for you!"

Shivers seized the Turkish pig;
He yelled out a summons:
"Oh Turks, if you believe in the Law,
Save me, the luckless one,
For the infidels have strangled me!"
Further the pasha ordered:
"Where is our blackamoor?"

Një harap me karabinë	A moor with a carbine
u ngulë e shtroj synë.	Kneeled and took aim.
Goditi bajrakn' e mirë,	He struck the goodly banner,
Marko Boçari shahinë!	Marcos Botsaris the falcon!
Erdhi Kosta vet i tretë.	Kostas himself came with three others.
"More shokë, gjithë erdhët?	"Hey, comrades, have you all come?
S'prit të vinja edhe unë?	Didn't you wait for me as well?
Vriti, shokë, Shqipëtare	Kill, oh comrades, the Albanian
biru qënet, se më vrane.	Sons of dogs, for they have slain me.
Mermëni sa jam i gjallë,	Take me while I am alive,
më muarë plumbi ndë ballë!	The shot has struck my forehead!
Ç'të bëj, o, fukara,	What can I do for you, poor man
që mbetë ti pa vëlla?	Who is left without a brother?
O, shokë, qajmëni hallë!"	Oh comrades, mourn the loss!"
U hodh i puthi në ballë.	He placed a kiss on his forehead.
U dëgjua anëmbanë:	Hither and yon it was related:
"Vrane Marko kapetanë	"They have slain Marcos the captain
që e kish kahuri të parë;	Who was first among the infidels;
pa të s'e bën' dot nizanë."	Without him they would not war."
Djemt e Sulit me vulë,	The renowned sons of Souli
shahin mbë dor' e prunë.	Bore the falcon in their arms.
Mu ndë Mesollongj e shpunë.	Within Missolonghi they carried him.
E shpunë ndë Mesollongj	He was brought to Missolonghi
t'a shërojnë, po s'shpëtoj.	To be nursed, but they could not save him.
Mesollongji u helmua	Missolonghi was embittered
e derdhi lotët si krua.	And shed tears like a fountain.
Mesollongji, ndaj të thonë:	Missolonghi, they will ask you:
Ku e ke Marko Sulonë	Where do you keep Marcos the Souliote
që lëftoj si pat zakonë,	Who fought as was his custom
gjithë me kordhë në dorë?	Always with his sword in hand?
Mesollongj ia bënë varrë	Missolonghi was his grave
me Qirjakul e Normanë.	With Kyriakoulis and Normann.
Mbeti derëziu,	Unfortunate he became
e bëri vetiu.	By his own deed.

Brilliant as this triumph must be regarded, it was the most dearly bought of all those acquired by regenerated Greece," a contemporary American historian of the Revolution wrote.[57]

> Though unblessed with the advantages which science and education bestow, Marco Bozzaris was endowed with all those manly virtues and that simplicity of character, which are only to be found in the heroes of Plutarch. His conduct from early life, whether in his capacity of citizen, patriot, or soldier, had excited the hopes, and won the admiration of the whole Greek people. Surely the last act of his life will bear an advantageous comparison with the most envied moment in that of Leonidas, or the hero of Mantinea!

[57] John L. Comstock, MD, *History of the Greek Revolution,* New York 1828, p. 276.

Greece will long have to deplore this irreparable loss. Yet it would have been impossible to die a more glorious death; and, however slender the hopes of replacing such a man may be, the event cannot fail to exercise a most salutary effect on those who are left to sustain the contest; while, if antiquity could boast a name, which has served as a never fading illustration to poets, orators, and historians, modern Greece may safely put forth that of Marco Bozzaris, as being scarcely less entitled to the palm of immortality.

It is no vain boast that, in the tragic days ahead and long afterwards, Missolonghi would be asked: "Where do you keep Marcos the Souliote?" This question, early in January 1824, was on the lips of an English poet who arrived at Missolonghi for a touching reunion with his beloved Souliotes and with an offer of his life for the Greek cause. After paying his respects at Marcos' grave, Lord Byron addressed himself to the impossible task of welding a regular army of the turbulent Souliotes—a task favored by neither the circumstances, the character of the men nor his own lack of military experience. As an Englishman, Byron left a mark upon his native literature. As an unselfish volunteer in Greece's fight for freedom, he left an indelible impression that is acknowledged by every Greek to this day. And, when illness slew the illustrious friend of Greek freedom a few short months later, he was laid to rest beside Marcos—later to be transferred to his native heath.

Missolonghi itself, despite all odds, continued to hold its besiegers for two years more. Its final act of defiance was against the combined might of the Ottomans and the troops of Mehmet Ali of Egypt led by his son Ibrahim Pasha. This latter force, moving up powerful artillery from Krioneri, pounded Missolonghi for three days in February 1826 "and afterwards for 15 days at intervals.

> By this tremendous cannonade, with such heavy ordnance, those parts of the town which had escaped previous attacks, were nearly battered down, but the garrison were still by no means disposed to listen to any terms their enemies chose to offer, though in great want of provisions, which the Turkish blockade had prevented their receiving.[58]

On March 6, the island of Vasiladi in the harbor of Missolonghi was stormed and taken by the besiegers under Ibrahim's brother-in-law, Hüsein Bey. Antolicon, another island point to Missolonghi's approaches surrendered a few days later, but the garrison on still a third island, Monasteri—75 men—succeeded in repelling the enemy and "no less than 1,500 Turks and Arabs perished on this occasion, and among them Hüsein Bey, without exception the best officer in Ibrahim's army."[59] An

---

[58] *ibid.*, p. 377.

[59] *ibid.*

ultimatum of surrender was communicated to Missolonghi's garrison and was spurned by its defenders who informed the admiral of the Ottoman fleet that he should address his request to the revolutionary government instead.

Miaoulis' Greek fleet now made repeated unsuccessful attempts to break the iron ring of Ottoman vessels blockading the starving town that refused to give in. With the failure of the last such attempt, the populace of the town was reduced to desperation.

The final decision of the "free men under siege"—as the defenders of Missolonghi have been called since—was taken on April 22. All received Communion from the bishop of Rhogous and, a few minutes after midnight, the gates of the town were silently opened. From the night-shrouded town, all the able-bodied—military and civilians, men, women and children—marched in stillness right into the mouths of the Turkish cannon. The enemy opened direct fire and 500 fell, the rest escaping to the hills. The sick and the wounded in the town awaited the crimson dawn when the enemy—Albanians, Turks and Arabs—marched into the shrine of liberty and commenced to massacre, pillage and rapine.

Just then, a roar shook the town as mines which had been laid beforehand were exploded—killing the surviving defenders and many of the enemy as well. About 150 men and 3,000 women and children, nonetheless, were carried off by the Turco-Albanians to Arta and Preveza and there sold into slavery.[60]

While these events were being enacted on land, a duel no less grim was being fought in the azure waters of the Aegean Sea and among the myriad little Greek islands that bedeck it. Today the summer playground of American and European tourists, the Albanian-speaking island of Hydra was then the bastion from which the men and ships of unshackled Greece came forth.

Hydra before the Greek Revolution had been the capital of a maritime confederacy whose ships were known from Smyrna to far-off Boston and New York. Much of the Ottoman Empire's sea trade was a monopoly of these precursors of today's Greek shipping tycoons. This fleet—the combined merchantmen of Hydra, Spetsai and Psara—was placed at the disposal of the Greek struggle for freedom.[61]

Both in the politics and battles of the Greek Revolution, these men

---

[60] For a stirring tribute to the memory of Missolonghi's last days, see Dionysios Solomos, "Free Men Besieged," in *op. cit.* pp. 225-282. Folksongs in Greek recounting the exodus from Missolonghi are to be found in Demetrius Petropoulos, *op. cit.* p. 170 and Speros Mouselimes, *Folksongs of Epirus: Region of Souli, in Epeirotike Hestia*, Vol. 12, No. 131, March 1963, pp. 219-220, Ioannina.

[61] See Constantine Paparrhegopoulos, *Condensed History of the Greek Nation*, Athens 1955, pp. 612-632.

were among the leaders. George and Lazaros Coundouriotes, Andreas Miaoules, Lazaros Panagiotas, George Sachtoures, Anthony Kriezes, Basil Boudoures, Demetrius Voulgares, Lascarina Bouboulina, are all names made immortal in modern Greek history.

The counterparts of the Greek Epirotes who spoke the same tongue and were fired by the same zeal on land, the "wooden ships and iron men" of these islands went down in history as modern Greece's first fighting navy. Their task was to bring to a halt a combined Turco-Egyptian fleet which, jumping from island to island in the Aegean, unleashed garrisons of Turkish, Arab and Albanian Moslem butchers who fell with ferocity upon often peaceful and unarmed islanders. Survivors of the inevitable carnage ended up on the slave blocks of Arabia and North Africa. Such was the fate of the island of Chios on March 10, 1822, and it horrified the world.

The provocation was the attempt of the islanders of Samos to persuade the Chians to join them in the fight for freedom. But let us hear the story as it was told to a shocked United States Congress in January 1824 by the honorable representative of the Commonwealth of Massachusetts, Daniel Webster:

> . . . the island of Scio, the most favored island in the archipelago, an island the peculiar property of the sultans, the slightest taxed, the most wealthy, the most refined, the most literate spot in all Greece, where were libraries such as few states in this union possess and where ease and elegance had their favorite seat, became the theatre of a massacre such as is not to be paralleled in the history of the world.
>
> The inhabitants of Samos, jealous at the comparative prosperity of this island, landed, drove the Turks into the town, and were joined by some of the country people of Scio.
>
> The Turkish fleet lately reinforced from Egypt, happened to be in the neighborhood, they landed and burnt the city, and when the slaughter and burning was over, out of 140,000 inhabitants, 900 only were left alive.
>
> Forty thousand women and children, inhabitants of the island, were sold at Smyrna into perpetual slavery. A month after, when the ashes of the burnt city were cold—did they hang 35 Greeks at the yardarm, and slay 85 more who had been given as hostages from the town. Ten more hostages were hanged in Constantinople—700, who voluntarily surrendered, were all shot down; 800 others, about whom they got into dispute, were murdered in the same manner.
>
> And, Sir, on the wharves of Boston did I see the utensils from the hearths of that polished, refined and literary people, selling for old copper. Numbers of children, all of whose relatives had been slaughtered, were picked up by the merchants in the Mediterranean, and some of them are now among us.[62]

[62] See David M. Robinson, *America in Greece, a Traditional Policy,* New York 1948, p. 86.

It was not until June 6 that the Greek fleet of Constantine Canares got the opportunity to revenge this frightful deed in an encounter on sea that cost the life of the enemy admiral, Kara Ali. The massacre and this encounter, like a salute from the "falcons of the hills" to the "eagles of the sea," is commemorated by the Albanophone Greeks of Epirus:

21.

Ferman ndë gjithë Turqi:
Fëjen një pasha firmanli
mbledh asqer ndë Shqipëri,
të dalë një për shtëpi.
U mbush bota me hasi.

An order to the whole of Turkey:
An outlaw pasha under ban
Has raised an army in Albania,
A man from every house.
The world has been filled with rebellion.

Sulltani dha prostaji:
"Kapetan në det kam ty,
o, kapllan, o, Karali!
Hidhu nisi mbi nisi!
Vuru zjar, digji si mi,
po rruaju nga ca gjemi."

The sultan gave a command:
"You are my captain of the sea,
Oh tiger, oh Kara Ali!
Throw yourself from isle to isle!
Set them ablaze, burn them like rats,
But guard yourself from certain ships."

Thotë Kapetan Kostandi:
"As aman, o, Karali!
Hioti s'ka faj; nuk di
seç bënet në Shqipëri.
As tundet, mbë vënd rri.
Mos e prish ndë je njeri,
ndë je pasha sojlli!

Quoth Captain Constantine:
"Mercy, oh Kara Ali!
The Chian is not at fault; I know not
What has been done in Albania.
None have arisen, they sit in their place.
Destroy them not if you're a man,
If you're a pasha of pedigree!

"Qën i qënit Osmanlli!
Nëm paç! Me çilimi
gjete të bëç trimëri?
Mbi njerëz pa fuqi
u vu zjarr e i bën hi?
Ktheu prapë në gjemi!
Këtu gjeta gjak të pi!"

Ottoman dog of dogs!
Damn you! With infants
Found you a way to be brave?
Upon helpless persons
Do you set fire and make them ash?
Turn back to your ship!
I have arrived here to drink blood!"

Natën që ra të flij,
i u pagua zullumi i tij
derr i derrit Karali!

At night when he lay down to sleep,
He paid for his crime,
The pig of pigs Kara Ali!

O, Kapetan Kostandi,
me kadale, me kupi
ju fute ndënë deti
e i ndeze po si qeri.

Oh Captain Constantine,
Slowly, by oar
You placed yourself beneath the sea
And you lit them up like a candle.

Karauli sokëllin:
"Jangën var! Po ngrehuni!
Na xhuriti gjarpër i zi
e s'e pam dot as me sy!"
Kur digjoj pashaj i zi,
thirri: "O, trima të mi,
qasni pranë një gjemi,

The lookout gave a cry:
"A blaze! Rouse yourselves!
The black serpent has burned us up
And even our eyes did not sight him!"
When the blackened pasha heard it
He shouted: "Oh my braves,
Bring a rowboat nigh

po s'kemi shpëtim, vallahi! *Posa mundni ikni!"*	For there's no saving us, by Allah! Let all who can escape!"
Keceu brënda në gjemi, *po katarti i ra mbi.* *Me kaq gjem, me zi* *e rrëmbeu Muhameti.*	He stepped down to the boat But the sail fell upon him. In such a state, with misgivings Mohammed seized him.
E sulltani ra mbë zi; *kreu një ferman të ri.*	And the sultan fell into mourning; A new order issued he.

Kara Ali was dead, but the duel at sea continued. On June 7, 1824, 3,000 Albanian Moslems were unleased upon the island of Kasos. Of the island's 7,000 inhabitants, the men and all the aged were put to the sword, while 2,000 boys and girls were seized by the Albanians and sold in the slave marts of Alexandria.[63]

On the morning of June 20, 140 Ottoman ships let loose a force of 14,000 men under Hosref Pasha upon Canares' native Psara.[64] In addition to its 7,000 inhabitants, the island's population had been swelled to 30,000 by refugees from surrounding islands and the coast of Asia Minor. Psara fell after a day's bloody fighting. When it was all over, only 3,000 Psarians had escaped slaughter, while 17,000 of the refugees were either put to death or sold as slaves. About 100 small craft fell into enemy hands.[65]

On land, the fall of Missolonghi opened the way to an inundation of Thessaly and Acarnania by enemy troops, while the arrival of the Egyptian forces of Mehmet Ali in Crete and the Peloponnese in large numbers assured the Albanians and their imperial master that the luckless revolt of the infidels would soon be crushed.

Far from united politically, the Greek leaders fell into dissentions that appeared to some observers to approach a state of civil war. Thus, the dark years of 1825-27 seemed to spell the end of a desperate break for freedom that had failed. But it did not fail, for even then the Greeks struggled on. With the tragic end of Missolonghi, the eyes of the world turned to another siege of a town far more famous than the Aetolian fishing port and soon to become the capital of free Greece—Athens. While John Gouras held Athens—aided by men such as Costas Lagoumtzis the Chormovan, whose skill in tunnelling and mine-laying came into precious

---

[63] Paparrhegopoulos, *op cit.,* 645-646. The folksong relating to the massacre at Kasos will be found in Petropoulos, *op cit.,* p. 169 (Vol. I).

[64] Although born on Psara, the commander of the fleets of Hydra, Spetsai and Psara was the youngest son of Nicholas Th. Spelioteas or Canares, a native of Parga in Epirus who had settled on Psara. See especially Angelos N. Papakostas, "Tradition Respecting the Descent of Constantine Canares" in *Neos Koubaras,* Vol. I., 1961.

[65] Paparrhegopoulos, *op. cit.,* pp. 646-648.

use—the outcome of the struggle was far from certain. In August 1826, Fabvier, the French officer who urged the deployment of regular troops had fallen out with Karaiskakis who was commander of the Epirote and Thessalian irregulars and had withdrawn to Salamis.

Some captains followed Fabvier, but, realizing that Karaiskakis—if defficient in European tactics—understood the foe somewhat better, they returned to him and Karaiskakis was enabled to regroup a force of 5,000. The besieged in Athens, who had their stronghold on the heights of the Acropolis continually called for aid and two attempts—on September 12 and 27—were made to relieve them. Both failed.

The following song, perhaps composed by a defender of the Acropolis, recalls these pleas for help. Although a song from the Greek side of the battlements, it speaks of "that Çelo Picari of ours." Why "ours" we shall explain in its place. Gouras' nephew mentioned here is John Mamoures.

22.

Kalaja ndë gerc Athinë	At the fort on Athens' hill
ç'e rrethosinë dyzet mijë,	Which was girded by forty thousand.
ky Çelo Picari ynë	That Çelo Picari of ours
lëfton Gura me të nipnë.	Battles Gouras and his nephew.
Gura dërgon për imdat:	Gouras sends for aid:
"Të vish, o, Karajshkaq,	"Come, oh Karaiskakis,
se unë kalanë s'jap	For I shall not give up the fort
sa të kem një pikë gjak.	While I have a drop of blood.
Ta marr Moraiti i nderit;	Let the honorable Greek take it;
s'jam muhip i Pejgamberit!	I'm not the Prophet's disciple!"

And, while the position of the besieged was desperate, that of the besiegers was little better. The Gheg mercenaries, in particular, had good cause to be bitter. At stake for the Epirote Moslems were privileges and feudal estates. The Ghegs, however, fought in a strange land where they had never been master and which was too poor for either booty or future prospects. To hear their plight, we must descend from the glory-drenched height of the Acropolis to the Ottoman camp below, where this song doubtless originated:

23.

Ori More, e zeza More,	Hey Greece, you blackened Greece,
sa shumë trimat ti na i morre?	How many braves did you take from us?
Shumë nonat na i verrbove;	Many of our mothers have you blinded;
shumë babat na i rrxove;	Many of our fathers you have executed;
shumë vllazninë na e vetmove;	Many of our brothers have you left lonely;
shumë motrat na i qyqove;	Many of our Sisters have you left like cuckoos;
shumë gratë na i vejove.	Many of our women have you widowed.
Do ta shkrujm' nji letër t'gatë.	We will write a speedy letter.
Do ta çojm' n'at vilatë.	We will send it to the province.

Le ta knojnë hoxhallartë.　　Let the hodjas read it.
Le ta knojnë letrën gratë.　　Let the women read it.

Në bvet nana ç'ka â mâ lirë,　　If mother asks you what is cheapest,
kryet e maces nji talirë.　　The head of a cat one thaler.
Në bvet nana ç'ka po bajmë,　　If mother asks you what we do,
misht e kalit po e hamë.　　We eat horsemeat.
Në bvet nana ç'ka po shtrojmë,　　If mother asks you what we spread,
jastik t'gurit na po 'ndojmë.　　We put a stone down for a pillow.

Kur na bjen mënd për nana,　　When we bring to mind mother,
dalim e kqyrim ka shkon hana.　　We go look where the moon sets.
Kur na bjen mënd për baba,　　When we bring to mind father,
dalim e kqyrim ka shkon vada.　　We go look where the ditches run.
Kur na bjen mënd për motra,　　When we bring to mind sister,
himë në shpi e rrimë në votra.　　We enter the hut and sit by the hearth.
Kur na bjen mënd për thmi,　　When we think of the children,
shkojm' e himë me kamë në hi!　　We go throw ourselves in the ashes!

In such straits, the Ottoman forces were as much in need of supplies and troops as the Greeks. One after another of the most able Albanian officers fell in this strange siege at the birthplace of Western civilization.

The following Moslem song refers to Muhtar Qafzezi whose native village in the Erseka (Colonia) district of Northern Epirus numbered 299 Moslems and 256 Christians before World War II.

24.

Ju, o, shpezë që fluturoni,　　Oh, ye swift of flight,
në Athinë të qëndroni.　　Gather ye in Athens.
Myftar Bejnë të ma zgjoni.　　Awaken Muhtar Bey for me.
Tre taborëve t'u veshtroni.　　Behold three encampments.
Të përpjetën e Siçanit[66]　　On the slope of the Museion
vetëtin kordh' e Myftarit.　　Sparkles the sword of Muhtar.

Ndë Siçan thurtur me gurë　　On the Museion strewn with rock
janë mbylltur kahurë.　　Are locked the infidels.
Ndë Siçan thurtur me trarë,　　On the Museion strewn with columns,
o, burrë-o, fustanëbardhë!　　Oh men, white fustanellas!

Myftar Bey, Myftar Vojvoda,　　Muhtar Bey, Muhtar Voyvoda,
ku i lë të shkretat hoda?　　Where did you leave the barren mansions?
Qafzezaz, o, të zi,　　Oh blackened men of Kiafzezi,
u shuatë e u bëtë hi!　　You were extinguished and became ash!

It was to the lot of Muhtar Bey's kinsman that a key military mission fell. Mustafa Bey Qafzezi was ordered to hold the area around Mount Parnassus clear so that Ottoman troops could move down in a sweep and relieve the besiegers of Athens. The flower of the Albanian troops,

---

[66] Sigan-Setze-Seggio (Throne, It.), was the name which had been applied since venetian times to the hill facing the Acropolis and crowned by the monument of the descendant of the Hellenistic kings of Commagene, C. Julius Antiochus Philopappus.

Mustafa Bey's force was to encounter the flower of the enemy Greeks in the first of a series of moves that would determine the fate of Attica. If Karaiskakis could dislodge Mustafa Bey, Athens was saved. If not, the consequences were a defeat from which the Revolution might never recover.

In Athens, the defenders were temporarily left leaderless by the death on September 30 of Gouras who was felled by enemy shot in a skirmish on the battlements. It was not until October 11 that Karaiskakis was able to send 450 men to beef up the garrison to which he designated Nicholas Kriezotis as commander.

Karaiskakis took with him the combined forces of 94 captains—many of them from Souli, Chimarra and other regions of Epirus—to meet the foe at Arachova. But first he sent ahead two of his captains to that point with 500 men, while a third was ordered to block the road from Arachova to Salona. At this point in the operation, Mustafa Bey made a tactical mistake. Fearing entrapment, he withdrew from the town of Arachova and sought stronger positions in the surrounding area at the foot of Mount Parnassus. Several days later, with other Greek captains at Zemeno blocking and scattering a force sent to strengthen Mustafa, Karaiskakis threw in his main force.

Mustafa offered to discuss withdrawal and sent his representatives, Hodo Leka and Sylejman Toska, to meet with John Roukes and Christopher Perrhaebus acting for Karaiskakis. This was a feint on the part of Mustafa Bey and his staff, which included his brother, Karafil Bey, Asllan and Elmaz Beys and the lieutenant of Kütahi. Negotiations broke down and a seven-day battle ensued. Badly outmaneuvered, the Albanians made a break on November 23, advancing sword in hand. During this engagement, Mustafa Bey was killed in battle by a pistol shot. In the confusion that followed, the Albanians were decimated and 700 Ghegs abandoned ranks and fled in the direction of the Jerusalem Monastery nearby. Half of them survived.

This victory was followed by equally brilliant successes by Karaiskakis at Tourkochori and Distomo as Ottoman hopes of a speedy end to the Greek rebellion began to fade for the moment. These events are the basis of the following Moslem ballad which ends on a curious note. When the handsome Mustafa Bey's body, along with that of his brother, were found, Karaiskakis sent the heads to the Greek leaders who included the fighting widow Lascarina Bouboulina. The anonymous Albanian bard—stretching poetic license a bit—imagines Bouboulina, whose hatred of the Turks made her the amazon of the Revolution as mourning his death because his beauty was such she would fain have married him!

25.

Athinë, e mjera Athinë,
del e shih asqer që vijnë.
Musta Beau me Dramallinë
sjellin gjithë Shqipërinë.
Që nd'Athinë e nd'Allamanë
janë shumë kapetanë.
Frikën Musta Beut ia kanë.

Musta Beu ka Livadhinë;
Taria lëfton Athinë.
Mun të kroj përmbi Rehovë
gjithë bajrakët u mblodhë.
Bie shi e bie dborë.
Musta Beu ndërton taborë.

Kush i shkeli malët e lartë?
Musta Beu pistollë artë!
Kush i shkeli malët me dborë?
Musta Beu fustanëhollë!

Çështë kështu, o, Musta Bej?
Nëndë ditë muhasere
pa bukë e pa xhephane.
Na vranë e na bënë dhe.
Ti, o Musta Be Misiri,
pretë ndihmë nga veziri?
Ndihmë s'ka, nga të të vinjë?
Tare Çuti mbet' Athinë.

"O, shokë, na vjen imdati
Hysen Beu nga Bozhigradi!"
More Hysen Be Devolli,
plastë lopa që të polli
edhe demi që të mbolli!
Hysen Beu ndihmë s'na solli.

Ti, moj kul e Livadisë,
ku ke trimn' e Shqipërisë?
"Ku t'a di, ah un' e mjera?
Ndë Rehovë e fryri era.
U vra beu vetull-hollë.
U vra dhe Thodhor Ollani.
E goditi Kapetani."

"Sihariq, moj Bubulinë,
na vranë Qafzezinë!"
"Pse më thatë këtë fjalë?

Athens, luckless Athens,
Come out and see an army coming,
Mustafa Bey and Dramali
Bring all of Albania.
In Athens and in Alamana
Many are the captains.
They fear Mustafa Bey.

Mustafa Bey holds Livadia;
Tare battles Athens.
At the fountain above Arachova
Every standard was gathered.
It rains and it snows.
Mustafa Bey makes his camp.

Who climbed upon the mountains high?
Mustafa Bey of the golden pistol!
Who climbed the snow-clad mountains?
Mustafa Bey with the fine kilts!

What is this, oh Mustafa Bey?
Nine days under siege
Without bread and without supplies.
They have slain us and cast us to earth.
You, oh Mustafa Bey of Egypt,
Expect help from the vizier?
There's no help, from whence is it to come?
Tare Çuti remains in Athens.

"Oh comrades, our aid is coming,
Hysen Bey from Bozhigrad!"
Hey Hysen Bey Devolli,
May the cow that bore you burst
And the calf that sired you!
Hysen Bey came not to our aid.

You, oh tower of Livadia,
Where do you keep Albania's braves?
"Ah, how know I, the luckless one?
In Arachova the wind scattered them.
Slain was the bey with the fine eyebrows.
Slain was Theodore Ollani.[67]
He was hit by the Captain."

"Congratulations, Bouboulina,
They have slain us Qafzezi!"
"Why do you tell me this word?

---

[67] Doubtless a Mirdite or Catholic Gheg, to judge from the name, otherwise unknown.

M'erdhi keq si për një djalë!
Të marr zën, kishin të gjallë,
burrë e keshë për të marrë;
t'a pagëzonja më parë
të zinja nga kjo farë!"

It comes evil to me as if for a son!
If he were taken, I wanted him alive,
I would wish to take him for a husband;
I would baptize him first
So I could contract with this tribe!"

Ububu! O, Musta Be,
seç të qa një zonj' e ve
penxhere mbë penxhere.
Shok ndë Shqipëri ty s'le!

Oh the sorrow! Oh Mustafa Bey,
That you are mourned by a widowed wife
From window to window.
A comrade in Albania is left you not!

Karaiskakis, too, was to fall. His death in a minor skirmish on April 22, 1827, left Greece bereft of a rough-hewn guerrilla commander whose intimate knowledge of the enemy's tactics had proved superb. Athens was not spared capture by the Ottoman troops and on May 6, 1827, the disasterous battle of Phaleron resulted in the transfer of Greek administration from the mainland to the island of Poros. For more than six years, Greece had fought and bled unaided by more than the good wishes of too distant America and a few private individuals in Europe, some of whom volunteered in the seemingly lost cause to fight and die on Greek soil. It was only when that cause seemed completely eclipsed that the screw of international diplomacy gave one small turn.

The accession to the Russian throne of a Tsar whose notions of Russian expediency were superior to the romantic nonsense of Holy Alliance was the turning point. The Russian plan was to fragment Greece into a series of tiny autonomous states and then to move on Constantinople. At this point, the British and the French reacted with a demand the sultan agree to an armistice and recognize the autonomy of Greece. The Russians joined in the signing of a treaty embodying these points in London on July 9, 1827.

Determined that victory and revenge—almost in sight—not be snatched from his hands, Mahmoud refused and the denouement of Navarino, in which the Turkish-Egyptian fleet was destroyed followed on October 20. The Tsar declared war on Turkey on April 26, 1828 and the Russian army occupied Adrianople where the Ottoman Empire signed a Russian-dictated treaty on September 9.

At the insistence of France and Great Britain, another conference with the Russians was called at London and the rump Greek state emerged. Confined to the Peloponnese, Attica and little else, this state was not the Greek nation, but an embryo. The majority of the Greeks were returned to Ottoman servitude to endure another century of struggle. But it was sufficient that this embryo lived. All Greeks turned to it with loyalty in their hearts and yearned for the day when the entire Greek nation would be free and united under its flag.

AN END — AND A BEGINNING
(1828-1830)

In January 1828, on the eve of Greece's statehood, an event demonstrated once more the unity of the nation and became the precursor of many such demonstrations in the course of the nineteenth and twentieth Centuries. Like Epirus, the island of Crete paid heavily for its part in the general struggle for Greece's liberation. A stepping-stone of Mehmet Ali's Egyptian armies which nearly succeeded in drowning the Revolution, it had been temporarily ceded to Egyptian rule in return for aid received by Turkey in crushing Greece. Its ruler, a Moslem Albanian—Mustafa Pasha—held the island in his bloody fist when an Epirote volunteer force headed by Hadjimichales Dalianes made a landing in an attempt to revive the struggle.

For many years, it was believed by some Greek historians that Dalianes was a native of the Greek-speaking town of Delvinaki on the present Greco-Albanian border. Mammopoulos, however, proves nearly conclusively that he came from the Albanian-speaking village of Delvinaki in the district of Premeti adding "Such is the glory of Pogonian Delvinaki that it will not be made less with the subtraction of one glorious son. As regards the bust of the hero, let it have the same impermanency as has the tomb of Basil of Dryinoupolis until the time when their weary bones will find their permanent resting places in the soil of their fathers."[68] Whether from Premeti or Pogoni, Dalianes was an indubitable son of Epirus—which is to say a son of Greece—who had made his mark with the forces of the Greek Revolution and had risen to the rank of commanding general of the Greek irregular cavalry.

In March 1826, he had taken part in a remarkable attempt at creating a military diversion for the Ottomans—in Lebanon, whose ruler was Al-Amr Bashir al-Shihab (1788-1840), "a crypto-Christian . . . whose aid Napoleon solicited in 1799 during his campaign against Syria."[69]

---

[68] Mammopoulos, *op. cit.* (Vol. II), pp. 70-71.

[69] Philip K. Hitti, *Origins of the Druze People and Religion, Columbia University Oriental Studies,* Vol. XXVIII, New York 1928, pp. 7, 8.

Acting on the plea for aid to the pro-Christian Druze governor of the
Lebanon, Kolettes had turned to Hadjimichales and the captains Nicholas
Kriezotes, Vasos Maurovouniotes and Stavros Liakopoulos. At his own
expense, Hadjimichales engaged 10 Spetsiote ships to carry 700 men to
Beirut where he landed to find that the governor was far from certain
that he would defy the Egyptians. In such circumstances, Hadjimichales
returned to Greece to fight beside Karaiskakes until that hero's death.
Such was the man whose landing in Crete was intended to renew that
island's struggle.[70]

A song—possibly a fragment of a longer ballad—has kept alive for
the Northern Epirotes the memory of their brothers who sacrificed themselves to free Crete:

26.

Në Gjirit u ngren' e vanë	To Crete they rose and went,
Vasua me Haxhimihanë.	Vasos and Hadjimichales.
Fora ç'e bën jataganë	To the fore were the sabres
përmbi Mustafa Pashanë.	Upon Mustafa Pasha.
Në portë të muaqemesë	At the courthouse door
rri vartur kryqi Moresë	Was set down the cross of Greece
e bënë besë me besë!	And they returned honor for honor.[71]

The Cretans, too, repayed "honor for honor" when, as volunteers, a
group took part in the liberation of Epirus in 1912 and rendered service
to the government of the Autonomy in 1914 until it was withdrawn. Its
withdrawal was requested by foreign powers who insisted it was no party
in the Epirote-Albanian dispute, although the Cretans and the Epirotes
thought otherwise.[72] Among the Epirote captains who took part in
Hadjimichales' ill-fated foray in Crete were Kyriakoules Polychrones of
Argyrocastron, Nicholas Tsoumbanes, Panagiotes Manoles, Tsakmakes,
Machaeras, Rhizos Zoes, Balaskas and George Maniates. The troop was
finally destroyed at Frangokastello at which Mustafa Pasha lost 1,700

---

[70] Two long Cretan ballads recounting the episode will be found in Aristides
Kriares, Cretan Songs, Chania 1909, pp. 96-102.

[71] Literally "made honor for honor", an idiomatic phrase meaning "they took their
revenge," for, to these Greek mountaineers, as for their Albanian foes, a foes attack
that went unanswered was an affront to the assaulted party's honor. Since it was
Greek honor that was wounded by Mustafa Pasha's brutality, only a Greek was
obligated to answer it. Hadjimichales and his Epirote braves undertook to answer it
by planting the Greek flag ("kryqi Moresë") before the very edifice in which the
tyrants' victims were condemned and where—exactly—the Ottoman practice had
been to display the severed heads of those so condemned. This must be understood
if those not steeped in Balkan tradition are to grasp the meaning of "honor for
honor."

[73] See AC, p. 84.

men. Hadjimichales was killed. Meanwhile, as Ali Pasha's former cohorts and his executioners were fighting the last round against the infidel upstarts, Sultan Mahmoud decided that his knife was sharp enough to finish what he had begun in 1808.

Following the precedent of Mehmet Ali's massacre of the Mamelukes, Mahmoud rid himself of the Janissaries "alla turca" when he replied to their defiant refusal to disband. The Janissary barracks in Constantinople were set ablaze and members of the corps were hunted down in the city's streets like animals. The *tekes* or monasteries of the Bektashis were padlocked and caretakers were appointed from the loyal Naksbendi order. This decree remained in force until 1839 when Mahmoud's son, Abdul Medjid II, only sixteen years of age, became sultan.[73]

The removal of the military mafia—predominantly Albanian in composition—was temporary, but the Janissary corps was gone forever. This fact, coupled with the intended establishment of a disciplined regular army, did not fail to impress Ali Pasha's former partisans who saw the proceedings as a deadly threat to their hereditary calling as armed irregulars. Even more suspect to Sultan Mahmoud was the loyalty of armed men who belonged to a proscribed religious order in which *takiye* or dissimulation was taught as a virtue.

Finally, a state had been established to which all of the Christians of Epirus, including the Moslem feudal lords, *çifçis* or tenant farmers, gave their true allegiance. Some of these men were shrewd enough to grasp the fact that what had been before would never be quite the same again, and they opened their own account with the infidels.

In 1829, the distinguished Chimarriote officer Spyromelios was serving as militia commander on the island of Euboia. He addressed a startling letter to Demetrius Hypsilantis, brother of the ill-fated hospodar. Hypsilantis was requested to forward it to Count John Capodistrias, the Greek head of state. It read:

> Eminent Generalissimo:
>   My father writes to me on April 20 from Chimarra that five or six aghas of Liabouria have compacted closely and under oath between themselves and have communicated to him the following:
>   1) That they are ready to raise the Greek flag in the province with a force of 4,000 men;
>   2) That they will surrender the fortress of Valona to the Greek government;

---

[73] One of the stringpullers behind the young sultan's throne was the *valide sultan* or empress mother who was said to have been a Bektashi herself. It was from Mahmoud's time that a Naksbendi dervish was regularly assigned residence in the principal Bektashi *teke* which directly overlooked Roberts College. It is gone now, with the formal abolition of the dervish orders by Kemal Atatürk. Only the cemetery remains.

3) That they will subordinate the whole province of Valona to the Greek state and govern themselves by Greek laws.

They request, therefore,

1) Religious freedom;
2) The preservation of their harems' honor;
3) 200,000 piastres in hand for their expenses.

If the Honorable Government is in accord with these offers of the aghas, they hope to receive a written confirmation from His Excellency the Governor[74], and they will then hand over their children and some of the notable aghas as surety.[75]

Because they have much confidence in me, they request I go there supplied with the government's letters to be addressed to Ilaz Aga Leka, Kadi Leka and the rest of the aghas. Finding myself, Eminence, under your command, I judge it my duty to address myself directly to you so that my petition will be directed to proper quarters.

"I do not know if the political situation will allow the Honorable Government to accept the above. You would not err, however, in the opinion of what and how many good things would be consequent to such assistance in Albania's midst and, of course, following the revolt of these aghas, Chimarra and all the rest of the Christian villages would be able to take up arms.

"I await the written reply of Your Highness and remain with all respect."

> June 2, 1829
> At the Teke of Thebes
> The dutiful Commandant of the Militia,
> S. Melios"[76]

Was there a reply to this remarkable missive? We shall never know unless, like the above, it turns up someday among the chaotically catalogued archives of the beginnings of the modern Greek state. Of one thing we may be reasonably sure—that the third essential term laid down by the Albanian aghas could not be met even if the Greek government favored the venture. In plain words, the Greek government in 1829 was financially stone broke.

But these intrigues of the aghas and beys could not and did not remain a secret from their peers who chose the sultan's side. A year later, Reshid Kütahi Pasha, now grand vizier, came to Monastir to preside ostensibly at a review of the forces he had led against Greece and to reward all to whom reward was due for their service. To this feast were invited about 400 Albanian beys and aghas, most of whom were

---

[74] i.e. Capodistrias.

[75] to give *rehem* or hostage as treaty surety was an Ottoman practice and at one time led to the imprisonment of all enemy ambassadors whenever the Porte was at war. The Albanian Moslems were making no extraordinary proposal.

[76] From the Vlachogiannes archives first published by Angelos N. Papakostas in the daily *Kathemerine*, Athens, February 26, 1947.

subjected to the same fate as their Janissary kinfolk in Constantinople. They were fired upon as they dined and few escaped. One of those who did not share the fate of his co-conspirators was an agha who had fought the Greeks fiercely at Missolonghi, Lepanto and the siege of Athens— Çelo Picari.

Accepting political asylum from the enemy against which he had fought hard and well, Çelo, "Tseliopitsaris" as the Athenians called him, became a citizen of Athens and a picturesque addition *to the visitors'* gallery of the Greek Parliament where he would follow the debates— clad in his native Lab costume—with the greatest interest. When the Labs rose again in 1847, he associated himself with a renewed plea for Greek intervention, and his name appears on a petition to King Otto signed by forty seven beys and aghas.[77] The majority of the Moslems of Epirus—who had not associated themselves with a conspiracy against their imperial master—saw in Çelo Picari a turncoat who had joined their common foe. This is their song:

27.

Kapetan Çelo Picari,	Captain Çelo Picari,
o, shejtan Veis Vasiari,	Oh devil Veis Vasiari,
ku shkoje të dridhej mali.	Where you went the mountains shivered.
Ndë Nebaht të vatë nami;	To Lepanto your fame has reached;
n'Athinë t'ungre pazari!	In Athens the marketplace raises you up!
Mesollongj seç u mblodhë.	At Missolonghi they gathered.
Gjithë zunë e të lëftojnë.	All began to seize and fight.
Katër mijë skllavë zunë,	Four thousands slaves they seized,
Çelos të falij ia prunë.	They were brought to Çelos to surrender.
E keqja përmbi kahurë!	What evil befell the infidels!
Pra ndë u arthtë koha kurrë,	Now, if their time were to come,
do na vrasin me gurë!	They would stone us to death!

Çelo Picari's dead comrades in arms had betrayed Ali Pasha to fight the Greeks for the sultan and, with Christian blood still wet upon their swords had offered them for sale to the Greeks. The hecatomb of Monastir was their fate. The Christian Epirote captains, who shared with these men a common ancestry in whose faith and nation they had remained faithful, had fought Ali Pasha in the hills and had fought them and their sultan to free their country. For those who survived, although their own birthplaces remained in bondage, there was the honor and satisfaction of having helped create and sustain a free Greek state.[78] Unto

---

[77] For the circumstances and the full text of that petition, see *AC*, pp. 48-50.

[78] Many Epirote veterans of the Greek War of Independence who would not return to their native villages which were returned to the rule of the sultan's cohorts

both, according to the saying, there "was rendered according to their works. Hallelujah!"

were granted modest tracts of land on former Moslem feudal estates in free Greece where they settled. Some settled in Euboia, Corinth and near Patras in the Peloponnese. A list of 129 Souliote families comprising 446 individuals settled by the Greek government in Lepanto (taken from the Vlachogiannes archives) is published by *Neos Koubaras,* 1962 (Angelos N. Papakostas: *The Drama of the Souliotes' Resettlement,* pp. 114-122.) The list is dated May 14, 1834.

OF HOPES AND DEEDS
(1832-1864)

The period from the establishment of the Greek Kingdom to the Balkan Wars was one of internal change in the Ottoman administrative system that succeeded in the abolition of few abuses and in the appearance of some new ones. The empire, as a whole, weighed itself down with the notorious Ottoman debt that forced it into receivership. By no means downed permanently by Mahmoud's reforms, the Albanian element in the corrupt Ottoman bureaucracy and military regained much ground. The sultans, beset by other problems, trod warily where Albania was concerned.

At the same time, the empire imposed conscription for the first time on the Christian element to which few compensatory rights were begrudgingly granted with one hand and withheld with the other. Whether in free Greece or in the major part of the country now back under Ottoman misrule, the Greeks regarded the period as a sequel to their eighteenth Century struggle for freedom with a difference. This was that the Greek state's territory was the sanctuary for all the Thessalian and Epirote *klephtai* who returned to their hills to harness the sultan's local representatives at every opportunity.

At the same time, the Greek mercantile class which had played a key role in the Ottoman Empire since 1453, now reestablished itself in Constantinople in all its former strength—and in free Athens as well. Both in arms and in the counting house, Epirus was well represented by sons who shared the dream of freedom for all of Greece.

Throughout this period, the clergy of the Greek patriarchate in Constantinople and throughout the empire, along with the empire's Greek mercantile class, counseled patience and, at least token, submission to the empire as they had before 1821. They knew only too well the weak economic and military state of Greece. But, exactly as before 1821, the rural Greeks chafed uneasily and looked longingly at their hidden caches of arms. Christians shivered at the thought of service with and under fanatical Moslems whose concept of *rayas* was one both of contempt and not unfounded suspicion of disloyalty. Christian resistance to Ottoman conscription in the period 1840-1850 gave birth to the following two Epirote folksongs:

67

28.

Që në Korçë e Tepelenë,	In Korytsa and Tepeleni,
të Kërshterët nizam s'venë.	The Christians wouldn't go into the army
Djemt e gjorë muarrën malë;	The barren lads took to the hills,
ikën as dihen ku vanë.	Fleeing to they knew not where.
Ky dhespoti i Manastirit,	That bishop of Monastir
ia fali djemt vezirit.	Surrendered the lads to the vizier.
Edhe dhespoti Perlepit	And the bishop of Perlepe
ia fali djemt dovletit.	Surrendered the lads to the empire.
O, dhespot, more dhespot,	Oh bishop, hey you bishop,
në nizam s'vemi dot!	We won't go into the army!

29.

Ra kuraja në Janinë.	The lot was drawn in Yannina.
Ku më gjet' mua të zinë?	Where did it find me, the blackened one?
Në male me trendelinë	On the hill with *trendelina*[70]
tek kullosi bagetinë.	Where I grazed the sheep.
Të zezat, o, dhënt e mija,	Oh my blackened sheep,
do t'i haj-o ulkunija!	The wolf pack is going to eat you up!

Large scale armed disturbances were linked to spasmodic Greco-Turkish tension and Russo-Turkish conflicts, although local flare-ups—particularly in the always touchy region of Chimarra, were not uncommon. As in the past, any attempt to assert Ottoman authority there was met by gunfire and any more general disturbance found the Chimarriotes ready to hoist the Greek flag. The type of local disturbance in that region is well illustrated in the following two songs. The circumstances giving rise to the first were as follows: An Ottoman gendarmerie captain at Berati was dunning an aged Chimarriote widow, Maro Andreou, for a sum he claimed she owed him. A fellow Vouniote villager, a shoemaker ("tsarouchas") took her part in the quarrel, waylaid the captain on the hill behind the village and shot him dead. What followed was inevitable. Doukas the shoemaker took to the hills, accompanied by a good many of the village lads ("Vouno has been set ablaze") and the provincial administration had another potentially explosive incident on its hands. Such incidents could rarely be drowned in blood. They could be resolved only by inaction or in long, drawn-out negotiations in Argyrocastron between the worried Ottoman authorities and the captains of Chimarra, usually represented by their *aza* or nominal administrator—always a Christian.

---

[70] Albanian for *trigonella corniculata* (bot.), a sweet-scented herb growing in profusion in Balkan hills and excellent for grazing sheep. It is also used in preserving and enhancing the taste of butter.

30.

Të shtunë, gjashtë sahati,	On Saturday, at six o'clock
Mbikodhim u bë fesati.	The murder took place at Mbikodhimi.
E bë Bon Dukë xhelati.	It was committed by Bon Doukas the killer.
Kush e njih Bon Carukanë?	Who has known Bon the Shoemaker?
Mbikodhim' e bë fesanë;	He did murder at Mbikodhimi;
vrau mulazim Beranë!	He killed the *mulazim* of Berati!
Tri dit në fsaka e lanë.	Three days they left him in the sagebrush.
Mudiri me ca xhandarë	The *mudir* with some gendarmes
e mbajtin vrapin në Himarë.	Stopped running at Chimarra.
Valiut tel i nganë.	To the *vali* he sends a wire:
"Vunoj ka ndezur zjarrë!"	"Vouno has been set ablaze!"

The most common manner of dealing with evildoers among the Labs when these occurred in the urban centers of the empire—and such instances involving these hill folk were not uncommon—was merely "sürgün"—exile to their native villages. Christian criminals could hardly hope to fare as well.

Two Chimarriote brigands are mentioned in the song below. One of them, Photos Michiles from the village of Koudesi, had shot dead the *kaymakam* or prefect of Smyrna (Izmir)—perhaps in a personal feud— and had fled to Chimarra with the authorities in pursuit. It is noteworthy that, such was the Chimarriotes' hatred of Moslem rule, they were lauded and their pursuers treated with contempt. It was enough that the pair were Chimarriote Christians. Their victim was a Moslem Albanian.

31.

Thanë duall' nga Izmiri,	They say they came from Smyrna,
thanë duall' në Himarë	They say there came to Chimarra
një juzbash me kacidhjarë.	A captain with some scrofulous men.
Kërkojn' Foton me Gavril Çalë.	They seek Photos and Gabriel Tsales.
Foto Mëhilli Kapetani,	Captain Photos Michiles,
në Stamboll të vatë nami:	To Stamboul your fame has gone:
"N'Izmir u vra kajmakami!"	"In Smyrna he killed the prefect!"
Shumë kapetanë janë	Many are the captains
fustangjer' e kambribardhë.	Girded with white cambric kilts.
Si Foto Mëhilli s'janë!	But like Photos Michiles there is none!

Alongside such local disturbances, the Crimean War (1854-1856) provided an opportunity for a new generation of freedom fighters to renew the contest in the hills. Thessalian and Epirote captains, procuring arms secretly in officially neutral Greece, crossed the arbitrary frontiers. Ranging the mountains of Olympus, the Pindus, Grammos and Smolika, they gathered local recruits and were received with ill-concealed enthusiasm by the restless *rayas*.

Official Greece was neutral of necessity, but the whole Greek people saw this ineffectual, costly and futile Crimean adventure from a pro-Russian viewpoint. It could not be otherwise while Russia fought an Anglo-French-Piedmontese alliance with the power that held two thirds of Greece in thrall. Correspondingly, the Moslem Albanians viewed this war with the infidel Tsar from the Turkish perspective, disappointed only at the inadequacy of Ottoman arms and provisions arising from dishonesty and peculation in Constantinople. These positions are reflected in the following Epirote ballad:

32.

T'a ngjiti, Moskov, t'a ngjiti	He attacked you, Muscovy, he attacked you,
Mustafa Pashë Gjiriti.	Mustafa Pasha of Crete.
T'u përgjegj posi petriti:	He gave you answer like a hawk:
"Qani male, qani gurë;	"Cry, mountains; cry, stone;
lëfton Turku me kahurë!	The Turk and the infidel battle!
Dolli ylli me bajrak;	The star goes forth with the flag;
me Moskovnë kemi gjak!	We have a bloodfeud with Muscovy!
Më kërkon për Krishtërinë	They demand of me for the Christians
Stamboll e Aja Sofinël"	Stamboul and Saint Sophia!"
Duall' edhe Kapetanë	There came forth as well the Captains
Kostë Rella e Kakaranxhë	Costas Rhellas and Cacarantzas
patrioti me Nataçnë.	The patriot with Natatsis.
Qirjakon kanë të parë.	Kyriakos they made their leader.
"Det-o lum anëmbanë,	"Misfortune hither and yon,
ju trima, ju kapetanë.	You braves, you captains.
Ngrihi, djem, të marrim malë	Up with you, lads, lets take to the hills
të mos na pjekin të gjallë.	So they won't roast us alive.
"O, dhespot, more dhespot,	"Oh bishop, hey bishop,
as e mbush ti kokën plot	Hasn't it entered your head
Frëngu na dolli prodhot	The Frank has become our betrayer
e ua ka Turkun për zot?"	And has the Turk for a lord?"
Ky Moskovi, trim me fletë,	That Muscovite, the winged brave,
lëftoj me pesë dovletë.	Fought with five kingdoms.
Malakofn' e bënë trokë,	The Malakoff was levelled,
po u mbajti kaq kokë!	But it took so many heads![80]
O, Moskov, o, perçgjatë,	Oh you long-haired Muscovite,
Turkun seç e bërë patë,	Thus you have subdued the Turk,
i dhe dërmën i dhe datë.	You made him fear, you made him tremble.
Çudite burrat edhe gratë!	You have made men and women marvel!

And the men and women of the Christian villages of Liountzi situated between Argyrocastron and Libochovo sang these songs of the deeds of their rulers' foes:

---

[80] A reference to heavy losses by Napoleon III's Crimean forces in successfully securing the heights of Malakoff at Eupatoria.

33.

Dëgjuat, ju Lunxhëri?
Dolli Moskovi në Vllahi,
fush e Gjergjovit u nxi!
Janë gjithë suvari,
zgjedhur-o delikalli.

Have you heard, oh Liountzi?
The Muscovite has entered Wallachia,
He has blackened the plain of Gheorghov!
They are all of them on horseback,
A choice of handsome braves.

Moj e shkreta Spaniadhë,
plot me banga, me dyqanë,
lëfton me Moskov Pashanë.

Hey, you barren Beardless Land,
Full of banks, of shops,
You're fighting with the Muscovite pasha.

34.

Sevastopull anë deti
ia vuri synë dovleti.
Një vënd fort' i mirë, shkreti
e qëllon me top nga deti.
Lëfton Englez e Francezi,
i gjori Moskov ç'e ndezi.

Sebastopol by the sea,
The empire fixes its eye on it.
A place well-strengthened, the barren one
Is struck by cannon from the sea.
The English and the French give battle,
The luckless Muscovite they've set ablaze.

O, Englez, o, derëzi,
vure sedër me Rusi.
O, mustaqerruari,
i vrari e i shuari!

Oh England, whose door is blackened,
You are vying with Russia.
Oh ye shorn of moustaches,
You are killed and you are wiped out!

Nikolla u tha një fjalë:
"Mençikofn' e kam si djalë
se lëfton me pashallarë;
u a vërvit topat pranë."

One word said Nicholas to them:
"Menchikoff is like a son to me
Because he fights the pashas;
He throws cannon shot upon them."

Gjashtëdhjetë gjeneralë
në Sevastopull u vranë.
Viktorisë kur ia thanë,
lidhi duart'e zu vajnë.
Malakofn' e muarrë
po të tërë shuanë.

Sixty generals
Were slain at Sebastopol.
When they told Victoria,
She crossed her hands and gave lament.
They took the Malakoff
But they were all wiped out.

35.

Këtë popullin e Rusisë,
që është i shum' si mizë,
kurrë Zoti mos ta prishë,
po ta shtoj' e ta stolisël
I ra në kokë Turqisë
që qe posi ulk, si bishë;
e zbriti e bëri gjizë!

This Russian people
Which is numerous like flies,
May the Lord destroy it not
But may He increase and bedeck it!
It has smitten the head of Turkey
Which is like a wolf, like a wild beast;
And she has been broken up to make
    cottage cheese!

Less than a decade later, 5,000 miles away, the United States too felt itself victimized by Napoleon III and his British friends and found cause to cheer the Tsar. Battling for its life, the Union saw French bayonets install a hostile regime in Mexico and the English eye evidence of the failure of Lincoln's naval blockade of the South with a view to diplomatic recognition of the Confederacy. It was then that a Russian fleet calling at San Francisco and New York was hailed as a precious friend. The return of the Greek captains to their lairs in Thessaly and Epirus met with no tangible success and they were forced to retire, but not before they had rekindled the Greek *rayas'* hope of liberation.

Two of the most important Greek guerrilla operations took place at Kalabaka and Metsovo. The former, situated in Thessaly at the foot of the strange rock formations crowned by the monasteries of the Meteora, holds the approaches to the plain. The latter is the key to the Epirus-Thessaly passes of the Pindus. How these assaults were viewed by the Moslem Albanians is displayed in two of their songs:[81]

36.

Kapetanët a Moresë
i ranë Turkut pa besë.
Van' e zunë Dumeqenë,
mbylle brënda Halim Bejnë.

The captains of Greece
Treacherously attacked the Turks.
They went and seized Domoko,
Hemmed in Halim Bey.

Ndë Çurp Papakosta vetë
na dolli vet' i tridhjetë.
Lëftoni, shokë, për besë!
Lum' ay që do të vdesë!

At Tsourpi Papacostas comes
Toward us himself with thirty men.
Fight, oh comrades, for the faith!
Blessed be he who is slain!

Kush dolli proto i parë?
Karafil Beu me Elmaznë!
Bir, o, bir Selim Hasani,
mbetë Mecovë si asllani!
Kallabakë, mbeç për lumë,
mbajtë Shqipëtarë shumë.

Who came forth first to lead?
Karafil Bey and Elmaz!
Son, oh son Selim Hasan,
You fell at Metsovo like a lion!
Kalabaka, may the river take you,
Many Albanians did you fell.

37.

Janinë ndë rrap i gjatë
mbyllurë shtatë bajrakë.
Dale, dale, o, Kallabakë!
Kallabaka shkëmb' i lartë
brënda mbyllturë Manjatë,
Morajitë xhufkë gjatë.
O, Kallabaka në gryk!

Yannina by the tall plane tree
Gathered seven standards.
Wait, just wait, Kalabaka!
Kalabaka the high crag
Before it gathered the Maniates,
The Greeks with tall caps.
Oh Kalabaka at the ravine!

Ndë një natë e ndë një ditë,
Abdyl Pasha me redifnë,
Çeloja me katër mijë,
mbi Kallabakë u vërvinë,
palla e jatagana qitnë.

In a night and in a day,
Abdyl Pasha with the reserves,
Çelo with four thousand,
On Kalabaka descended
Wielding sabres and scimitars.

[81] For Epirote folksongs in Greek covering the same events, see Athanasius Ch. Giankas, *op. cit.*, pp. 76-78, and Agis Theros, *op. cit.*, p. 42.

Kush u hodhi krejt ndë Petë?	Who charged ahead on Peta?
Çeloja me tetëdhjetë!	Çelo with eighty men!
"Haj, o, djemt, të hidhemi;	"At 'em, boys, let's fall on them;
të gjithë të vritemi!"	Let us all be slain!"

The captains' stand at Metsovo was disastrous and resulted in the partial destruction of that prosperous village.[82] Upon the withdrawal of the Turko-Albanian garrison in the first week of March, 1854, the Greek guerrillas under Theodorakis Grivas entered and, for a fortnight, the Metsovites celebrated as at a wedding. But, on a day sacred to them as Christians and as Greeks, the Albanian reserves ("redifs") returned and fell upon them.[83] In a three-day battle, the guerrillas were forced to withdraw toward Malakasi and the Albanian Moslems entered to burn and loot. The Metsovites, who paid so dearly for two weeks of freedom, had to wait another 58 years before their final liberation. The Albanian-speaking Greeks of Northern Epirus did not fail to mourn the plight of their Vlach-speaking Greek brethren of Metsovo at the hands of a common foe.

38.

Mecova gjithë sarajë,	Metsovo, all mansions,
të kisha kërcejnë vallë.	Throws a dance at the church.
Bejnë qeveri të madhë;	It had a great government;[84]
Turkun s'e pëshojnë farë!	They gave the Turk no mind!
Mecovë, e shkretë Mecovë,	Metsovo, barren Metsovo,
shum' u majtë, pra t'u hodhë.	Much you prospered, so they attacked you.
Të vunë zjarr e të dogjnë.	They set you ablaze and burned you up.
Të mali pa çkrirë bora,	On the mountain where the snows melt not,
pesëqind shtëpi Mecova;	Five hundred houses in Metsovo;
pesëqind shtëpi me radhë,	Five hundred homes in a row,
katërqind copë dyqanël	Some four hundred shops!
Një kull' e vogël mb'anë	A small tower at the edge
mbyllurë dy kapetanë,	Harbors within two captains,
Kiçoja me të vëllanë,	Kitsos and his brother,
ata që vranë Selamnë.	They who killed Selam.

[82] The native village of such benefactors of the whole of Greece as George Averoff and Baron Tositsa (former Greek Foreign Minister Evangelos Averoff-Tositsa is a descendent of both), Metsovo was rebuilt and regained its former prosperity. Its proud, Vlach-speaking inhabitants still, for the most part, wear their picturesque black costume (the "dimiti" and round cap) and yield to none in civic pride. Few mountain villages can boast of a high school, a public park and even a little zoo. Metsovo can!

[83] March 25, both Annunciation and Greek Independence Day. See Petropoulos, *op. cit.*, p. 222 for a song in Greek referring to the same event.

[84] Meaning its village council of elders.

In the north, too, the internal disturbances triggered by the Crimean War and aimed at preparing the way for the liberation of the Greek *rayas* took place only to be quelled. In one successful but inconclusive skirmish, a company of Albanians under Zalo Bey Burradani was put to flight with scarcely a shot fired.

39.

Në Konica joklama,	In Konitsa there's a call,
hajde Nexhip Beu, hajde!	Hurry, Nexhip Bey, Hurry!
Në Furkë shkelnë andartë,	At Phourka the guerrillas advance,
gjashtë shtatë kapetanë,	Six, seven captains,
Davelli me të vëllanë.	Ntavelis and his brothers.
Zalo Beu, një djal i gjatë,	Zalo Bey, a grown-up lad,
mbathi tumanët si gratë!	Donned drawers like the women!

The first of the following three songs refers to Captain Spyros Stoyas of Lower Labovon ("of Zappas"). The other two originate in the region of Korytsa which, until the Balkan Wars, was administratively part of the Vilayet of Monastir (western Macedonia). The third song relates how the rebellion in the latter sanjak was quelled by the calling out of the traditional "fire brigade," the Ghegs of Dibra and the Metohija. In this song, too, we find the involvement of a luckless captain from Chimarra (Spyros Chormovas) and volunteers from other parts of Epirus as well.

40.

Kush e bëri proto fora?	Who was first to charge?
Kapetan Spiro Labova!	Captain Spyros of Labovon!
Shqipëtarë, o, gunë bardhe,	Oh, white-capoted Albanians,
pse muartë përpjetë malë?	Why take ye to the hills?
S'e lëshon pallën nga dora,	You leave not sword from hand,
Lule more Spiro Stoja	Oh blossom Spyros Stoyas
me të shkretën të murrmen gunë,	Of the dark short cape,
me fustanen përmbi gjunjë!	Of the kilt above the knee!
Ç'u hodhe përmbi ordhisë,	How you threw yourself upon the horde,
u dhe datën Turqerisë.	Throwing fear into the Turks.
Ngreu, o, Spiro, nga varri	Arise, oh, Spyros, from the grave,
se të blegëron manari!	Your lamb calls out for you!
Tre plumba ndë ball i ranë;	Three shots struck his forehead;
trimat-o ashtu e kanë!	Thus is fated for the brave!

41.

Me dy jave Shkurt,	In the first fortnight of February,
të djelë mbë drekë,	Sunday at noon,
"falu, Naum, falu,	"Surrender, Naoum, surrender,
nga shkëmbi mos bjerë,"	Don't throw yourself from the crag,"
të thirri bimbashi,	The major called to you,
të thirri tri herë.	He called out thrice.

Seç të iknë shokët,
mbete vet' i tretë.
Seç tëengrinë duart,
s'zbrasnjë dot dyfeknë.
T'u sosën fishekët,
mbete me vezmetë.

Your companions fled,
You remained with three others.
Your hands froze,
You could not load the musket.
You ran out of bullets,
Your cartridge boxes empty.

Ç'u pshtolle me gunë,
u flake si shpesh.
More tatëpjetën,
u hodhe në lëndine.
Kapetan Naumi,
rrëfeve trimërinë!

You wrapped yourself in a cape,
You charged like lightning.
You took the downhill,
Throwing yourself to the valley.
Captain Naoum,
You emerged a brave!

42.

Pa pritë, moj Korç'e shkretë,
ia të vijnë treqind Gegë.
Gramoz muarrën **përpjetë;**
hidhën posi shigjetë.
Kostë Rella zu thërriste;
Spiro Hormova zu vise.

Just wait, oh barren Korytsa,
Three hundred Ghegs are coming to you.
They took to the heights of the Grammos;
They hurl themselves like an arrow.
Costas Rhellas gave a shout;
Spyros Chormovas took up his post.

Aliaj u hodh ndë **driza;**
njerëzit i duken miza.
"Dale, dale, o, Kostë Rella,
këtu ta gjetëm limerë.
Spiro Himarën t'a therë."

Ali threw himself in the forest;
His men swarmed like flies.
"Hold on, hold on, oh Costas Rhellas,
Here we've found your hideout.
They've slain your Spyros of Chimarra."

Që të Mart' e gjer të Shtunë,
kokën e Spiros Korçe e shpunë.
Kokën a Spiro Himariotit
e panë syt e Sulotit.

From Tuesday until Saturday,
They bore Spyros' head to Korytsa.[85]
The head of Spyros the Chimarran
Was beheld by the eyes of the Souliote.

The Crimean War ended. Greece did not intervene in Thessaly and Epirus and the fever of rebellion ran its course and subsided. But this did not mean that individual bands did not appear from time to time to harry the Ottoman authorities and raise hopes then seething near the surface. One such captain, who fell in 1862, was Androutsos Mourgatsis, a native of Nivitsa Boubari whose brave inhabitants kept his name alive in the following song:

43.

Gjashtëdhjet e dy seneja
ç'u vra Andruc Murgaç luleja!

In Eighteen Hundred and Sixty Two
Was killed Androutsos Mourgatsis the blossom!

Dolli hajdut nga Morea.
Në Sakun muzaqerea,
pas iu ngjinë paganea.

He emerged a guerrilla out of Greece.
At Sakouni was the gathering,
Behind him they came in hot pursuit.

[85] "From Tuesday etc.—i.e. it was paraded in the surrounding Christian villages for five days by his Moslem slayers as an example to the *rayas*.

Paganea pas iu ngjinë	Behind him came the hot pursuers
në male mbi Samarinë;	To the mountain by Samarina;
plumbat si vetëtimë.	The shots like lightning.

Kapetani ngjit borinë.	The captain sounded the trumpet.
Pritë për shok e s'munt t'i vinë.	He waited for his comrades who couldn't come.

Kapetani qan me lot:	The captain cried bitterly:
"Ç'u bëtë, o, Nivicjot?"	"Where are you, oh Nivitsans?"
Kapetani rri si pika.	The captain was downed like a bolt.
Ç'u bëre Andruc Nivica?	What happened to you, Androutsos Nivitsan?

But the Ottoman Empire and its Albanian creatures, whatever they might do on the mainland, could not prevent the Ionian Islands—Corfu and its six sister isles—from passing to Greece. Greece's first king, Otto of Wittelsbach, was dethroned in 1863 after the granting of a constitution and the dismissal of his Bavarian advisors failed to mollify the Greek people. In his stead, a Danish prince became King George I. A constitutional monarch, he took "My strength is the love of the people" as his motto and he called himself—although two thirds of the Greeks were beyond his nation's borders—not King of Greece, but of the Greeks. He took a Romanov princess to wife and England provided the dowry in 1864—the islands at the mouth of the Adriatic.

The Albanians understood that this could not fail to bring the Greek flag on Corfu within striking distance of Epirus. To them, it was all part of a Greco-Russian plot to destroy them and their Ottoman master. Thus they mourned:

44.

Qan dovleti nat'e ditë	Night and day the empire weeps
se ia rrethuan nisitë.	For it is hemmed in by the islands.
Moskovi dhe Moraitë	The Muscovite and the Greek
kërkojnë shtatë nisitë.	Demand the seven islands.
I duan se i kan' të tijtë!	They want them because they are theirs.

OF FAITH AND WORKS
(1864 - 1912)

Athena, that ancient protectress of the Hellenes, wore a double aspect. When beheld as the militant defender of her city's liberty, she was seen holding spear and shield, ready to battle the barbarian at the gates. But when worshipped as the Logos which sprang full-grown from the forehead of Zeus, her features softened. She was then the goddess of knowledge and the patroness of learning. The owl of scholarship found its perch upon her shoulder and, if she battled, it was with the barbarian in the heart of each of her votaries. Bandits and heroes, wars and rebellion, stud the tragic story of Epirus. But, were this the alpha and omega of the tale, the Epirotes—and Greece as a whole—would have been immeasurably poorer for it. And the story of Epirus' self-created Greek schools is the story of its self-made men—its immigrants.[86]

It is a story Americans, with their whole tradition of restless migration and "rags to riches" are best able to appreciate. But, comparing the American tradition and that of the Greek there is a difference, and it is an ancient one. Unlike the builders of the New World, Ulysses and his children always made the Ithaca from whence they started their final port of call.

Beginning in the mid-nineteenth century, the constant migration and return assumed larger proportions. Based since ancient times upon the paucity of tillable land and aggravated by the alienation of much of that land by a foreign conqueror, it was both curse and blessing. It was a blessing in that it allowed those whose wits were sharp and whose luck was good to afford themselves and their kin a standard of living the local economy could not afford. It was also a curse that made quasi-widows of wives and strangers of offspring, stripping villages of their menfolk in their prime of life. And there was no guarantee that luck would smile or, indeed, that a man might not be swallowed up by misfortune and death in a friendless clime.[87] While some men went far to lands "east of the Sun

---

[86] See especially *AC*, pp. 50-53.

[87] An excellent treatment of this is Alexander Ch. Mammopoulos, *Emigration and the Demotic Song* (Lecture addressed to the Epirotic Society of Athens, Nov. 11, 1964.)

and west of the Moon," most migrated to the surrounding lands of the Near East, Mediterranean, Central and northeastern Europe where the flow of migration had been directed since the fall of Byzantium.

The pattern varied little. One generation would succeed another abroad while the older generation returned to spend its declining years by its native hearths. After a young man received his first years of schooling in his village, he would be called for by his father abroad to learn his father's trade or profession. Should his father's means permit, he would complete his schooling abroad.

There were brief returns to the village where one was born—to wed, beget, baptize, marry off one's offspring, bury one's parents. Finally, there would be a last, long return to savor the fruits of one's labor as a son or sons abroad succeeded one. Great was the exultation of a whole village in the good fortune of a native son, but his initial departure was accompanied by tears and lamentation—as always—by the womenfolk. Later, when America opened wide its hospitable gates, these lamentations of parting included this land in their doleful threnody:[88]

45.

Ç'ish na dolli në gurbet i ri?	What new land abroad to us appeared?
Zjarr të marrë Ameriqi!	Go to blazes, America!
Na mblodhi djemt gjithë delikalli.	It gathered all our handsome youths.
Zjarr të marrë Ameriqi!	Go to blazes, America!
Benë nusat me duart në gji.	The brides remained with hand to breast.
Zjarr të marrë Ameriqi!	Go to blazes, America!
Qajnë, çupat me lot i zi.	Maidens weep with blackened tears.
Zjarr të marrë Ameriqi!	Go to blazes, America!
Vunë plakët çeberë të zi.	Old women don black kerchiefs.
Zjarr të marrë Ameriqi!	Go to blazes, America!

But the bright side of this migration more than compensated for many those black tears of parting. Villages that had made a livelihood at the edge of poverty became wealthy not by local privileges of exploitation or the spoils of war and brigandage—as was so often the case with their oppressors—but with the hard-earned gold honestly garnered in many lands by successful sons. Mansions were erected where once there were huts, for whole villages prospered in the good fortune of one or two native sons. The success of one meant jobs abroad for others who were thus afforded the same opportunities for enrichment. The instinct of mutual

---

[88] Very similar songs in Greek expressing the same sentiment will be found in Tarsoule, *op. cit.*, P. 135. and Evàngelos St. Tziatzios, *Songs of the Sarakatsans*, Athens 1928, p. 36.

aid was strong in these patriarchal, peasant-born merchants and bankers, shippers and manufacturers.

The most successful of these men were double benefactors. If they endowed schools in their villages—and this was the commonest philanthropy—they never failed to do the same—and more—in the Greek communities abroad and, especially, in the capital of a land some of them never saw—Athens. Thus, from one and the same man, time and again, Athens and an obscure mountain village in Epirus shared in the wealth emanating from far-off St. Petersburg or Khartoum.

One such man, born in 1800 in Labovon near Tepeleni,[89] which afterwards called itself "of Zappas," was Evangelos Zappas, one of the first great Greek philanthropists of the nineteenth century. His father, Basil, was a merchant, and Evangelos left Labovon at the age of 13. Many years later, now a renowned industrialist and landowner in Rumania, he related something of his young manhood in a petition addressed to the Greek consul general in Bucharest. The petition was a request for proper recognition of faithful service to his country from 1821 to 1830.[90] In it we learn that he was aide de camp to Marcos Botsaris, then served under Nicholas Panourias, John Gouras and Kitsos Tzavellas in nearly every major battle of the Revolution. He was, he said, wounded five times. His mother, who had remained in Labovon, was seized by Kütahi Pasha's orders and held hostage in an underground dungeon on Yannina's island in 1825. The Albanian detachment that seized her, headed by Kalo Bey of Argyrocastron, thoroughly looted and smashed his home.

This action, he continued, was taken in hopes "I would come out and surrender, but I ignored everything, mother and home, and kept unsullied my sacred revolutionary oath to my country which I shall keep to my very last breath. As witnesses to these sacrifices, he called in the petition upon his still surviving fellow veterans of the War of Independence—Kitsos Tzavellas, Spyromelios, Nicholas Panourias, George Dyovouniotes, Demetrius Lioulas, John Bairaktares, Papacostas Salonites and Nicholas Zervas. He signed himself simply "Evangeles Zappas from Labovon of Epirus." Behind that modest signature was a lifetime of achievement that would continue beyond the grave.

After the Revolution, Zappas went to the Danubian Principalities where he practiced first the humble calling of "practical doctor," but soon acquired a wheat mill. In time, his mills multiplied and he acquired much

---

[89] In 1908, the combined population of the twin villages of Greater and Lesser Labovon was 932, all Christian. This is not to be confused with the Labovan ("of the Cross") in the region of Argyrocastron.

[90] Full text of the petition (in Greek) is published in *Neos Kouvaras,* Vol. I, pp. 100-101.

land besides, becoming one of the wealthiest Greeks in Bucharest. During
his lifetime, he gave generously both for a Greek school in his native
Labovon and to the newly-formed "Olympic Committee" of Athens which
was planning an "exposition palace" and park. On his death on June 19,
1865, his fortune was estimated at 6,000,000 gold drachmas. Of this
legacy, 3,000 florins annually were earmarked for the school at Labovon
and other similar bequests while 15,000 florins annually were provided
for the exposition palace and park, known today as the Zappeion. The
rest of his fortune was left to his heir, his cousin Constantine, to revert
to the Zappeion endowment upon the latter's death. In 1869, in accordance with the terms of his will, Evangelos Zappas was reinterred in the
courtyard of the Greek school in Labovon.

His cousin, Constantine, continued and expanded the endowments. In
1875, he endowed Constantinople's Greek community with the Zappeion
School for Girls and also gave generously for educational purposes to
the Greek community of Adrianople. In his own native Epirus, he en-
larged the school at Labovon and endowed schools in Philiatae, Droviani,
Delvino, Premeti, Nivani and Lekli. A sum of 250,000 gold drachmas
was deposited by him in the National Bank in Athens to provide scholar-
ships for Greek agricultural students desiring to study in Europe. When
he died on January 20, 1892, the remainder of his fortune earmarked
for the "Olympic Committee" became involved in lengthy litigation in
the Rumanian courts and was never released for the purpose for which
it was intended. In listing the Greek school in Lekli, a curious fact
should be mentioned. Because the village was situated near the now
Moslem stronghold of Chormovo—which looked with jealousy at signs
of growing prosperity in a nearby Christian village—Zappas endowed,
at the same time, a mosque in Chormovo! The incident is recalled in
the following song:

46.

Zhapajt Vëllazëri,	The Zappas fraternity,
Kostandini në Vllahi,	Constantine in Wallachia,
mbushin Labovën me flori.	Have filled Labovon with gold.
Bëri kishë dhe shkolli;	They have created a church and school;
në Hormovë një xhami,	In Chormovo a mosque,
në Lekle një shkolli	In Lekli a school
të mësonj djemtë gramati.	To teach the children letters.

That the apprehension respecting the cupidity of the Moslems was
not unfounded can be seen from what later happened to Katerina, the
Zappas' niece, grandmother of the wealthy Dr. Karagiannes in the little
village of Terbouki.[91]

---

[91] Population in 1908: 185, all Christian.

One night, Shemo the brigand and his band descended upon the house and hacked the entrance door to pieces. Rushing inside, they found Katerina (Kato), a diminutive woman but brave as they come, standing upon a chest with an ax in her hand. She, too, was hacked to pieces and the house was looted. Meanwhile, the village was aroused and the bandits fled. One villager, Nicos Tephas, who had a crippled leg, took his double-barrelled hunting piece and climbed a tree. He called to Shemo who passed below and looked up. Then he blasted the bandit with both barrels. Shemo paid for his crime on the spot.

47.

Të Shtunë, aty në darkë,	On a Saturday, there at evening,
vatë Shemua me shpatë.	Shemo went with a sword.
"O, Kato, ne na paratë!"	"Oh, Katerina, give us the money!"
Katua hipi në karcellë;	Katerina climbed up on a chest;
me jataganë e therrë!	With a scimitar she was hewn down!
Tërbuq një fshat i pak;	A little hamlet is Terbouki;
burra trima e trima grat.	Brave men and brave women.
Duall të gjithë me shpat.	They all sallied forth with swords.
Nikua, kur morri haber,	Nicos, when he got the news,
"Shpejt, bimëni çiftenë!	"Hurry, fetch me the double piece!
Do të ze Shemos steknë!"	I shall set Shemo a trap!"
Vrave një pendarë grua;	He slew a two-bit woman;[92]
t'u hodhë koka në prua!	His head was tossed in the stream!

The Zappas' example was not unequalled nor unsurpassed. Many were Epirus' emigrated sons who left bequests of considerable size both in Epirus and in Athens, to say nothing of the Greek communities abroad. One who holds a special place in Epirote esteem is the late Christaki Effendi Zographos. Born in the village of Kestorati situated between Argyrocastron and Libochovo[93] on Dec. 6, 1820, the future national benefactor studied his first letters in his native village. For two years, he attended the Zosimaeon High School in Yannina and then went off to Constantinople to join his father. From a young partner in a small money changing stall at Galata together with a countryman, Michael Demos who died a short time after, Christaki Zographos became the leading banker and financier, the founder and head of the *Societé Générale Ottomane* and president of the Turkish capital's new—and sole—trolley company. Decorated by three sultans, he sat on the Imperial Board of Estimate and served as president of the Ecumenical Patriarchate's Clerico-Lay Advisory Board.

[92] Literally "a five para (Greek goes here) woman."

[93] Population in 1908: 284, all Christian.

When the Constantinople Hellenic Literary Society's first headquarters were destroyed by fire, it was Zographos who rebuilt them along more impressive lines and was named honorary president. But his aid to the society did not stop there. A £600 annual endowment to the society's scholarly publication and an annual £100 prize fund for Greek folklore studies awards, also published at his expense, were some of his gifts to the society. At the universities of Munich and Paris, he made 1,000 franc endowments for awards in Greek letters. He subsidized the Zographos Library of Classical Authors which began to issue its series in 1873. Other grants went to the Patriarchate's Theological School at Chalki (Heybeli Ada), and he was deservedly decorated with the Gold Cross of the Patriarchate by His Holiness Joachim III. The Zographeion High School at Pera and the Zographeion Girls School at Neochora on the Bosphorus were both products of his generosity. To the Greek education of his native Epirus, Christaki Effendi left the Zographeion Teachers School in Kestorati, for which he also provided an annual endowment of Fr. 27,600 for the education of sixty future village teachers.

48.

Mu të portë me sufa,	At the door with plastering,
brënda xhevahirë ka.	He has a jewel inside.
Brenda xhevahirë pati	Inside had a jewel
Hristaqi nga Qestorati.	Christaki from Kestorati.
Kreu monedhën të re,	He issued a new coin,
flori me katër qose:	A gold piece with four corners:
Në mesin e Qestoratit	In the midst of Kestorati
atje qe gjimnazin fshatit!	There was the village high school!

To Greece as a whole, as well as to Epirus, Christaki Effendi left one more gift—his son, George. A doctor of law and political science, George Christaki Zographos was the architect of agrarian reform in Thessaly, served in the Greek Parliament as deputy from Karditsa and became foreign minister in the 1909 cabinet of Demetrius Rhallis.

Upon the liberation of all Epirus in the Balkan Wars, he became the first Greek governor since Evrenoz Ghazi entered the city of Yannina in the 15th Century. But when Northern Epirus—whose true son he, too, was—became Albanian by Europe's fiat, he sped to Argyrocastron. There, he headed the government of the Northern Epirote Autonomy which rallied the Christian majority to a successful contest in arms that established a short-lived Greek state. That state, like Sam Houston's Texas Republic in our own country, yielded to its own motherland when Greek armies reentered a second time.

At Italian insistance, Greece was ordered out a second time in 1916 and the drama of Northern Epirus entered a stage from which it has yet to emerge. Returning to Athens after the dissolution of the Autonomy, George Zographos was again elected to the Greek Parliament. Not long afterwards, he left politics to become a National Bank executive save for a brief interlude as foreign minister in the Gounaris cabinet of 1915. He retired from the bank in 1917 and died of a longtime heart ailment on June 24, 1920. The regard for which Christaki Effendi was held by the folk among whom he was born is expressed in the following song celebrating his trip to Paris to attend the nuptials of his daughter, Theano, and Leonidas Deligeorges, who served as Greek foreign minister in the Deligiannes cabinet (1890-1892):

49.

Erdhi teli, shkronja pruri	A wire came, it brought tidings
n'atë vijë me plumis.	Along that winged way.
Thanë Deligjorgji zuri	They say Deligeorges held
dasmën; e bëri në Paris!	A wedding; he made it in Paris!
Nisemi, në kishë shkojmë	Let us start, to church we'll go
t'i falemi aty Zot.	To give thanks there to the Lord.
Theano, do të urojmë	Theano, we'll wish you well
për kurrorë që vë sot.	For the crown you don today.
Luaj, o, Zografo, luaj,	Begin, Oh, Zographos, begin,
luaj valle dhe këndo.	Begin to dance and sing.
Sikur jemi atje na quaj	As if we were there he calls on us,
"pi shambanj' e na kujto!"	"Drink champagne and remember us!"

In addition to his philanthropies, his countrymen had still another reason to look upon Christaki Effendi as their benefactor. It was not for nothing that he held high Ottoman honors and had a voice in the empire's finances. Such a man could—and did—interpose his power and influence against that often unchecked scourge, the Lab brigands. Such an instance is recalled in the songs below. Zographos' fellow villager, Koto Duda, was a provisioner in Constantinople. His wife, Catherine (Katcho), *nee* Giannakes, was in Kestorati with her seven children when the brigand Hamit Guga came calling. With her home undefended, she was ripe for looting and Hamit planned to make off with her and the children to hold for ransom. But the plucky woman was equal to the occasion. She offered the brigands spoonfuls of jam and plenty of *raki*. As the potent Balkan "mountain dew" went to their heads, Hamit and his boys began to sing and dance. This was her cue to sneak her children, one by one, out a back window. Then she followed. To her consternation, however, she found that her youngest, Tassos, was still inside. Unnoticed by the now completely soused Albanians, she reentered, seized the baby and fled to safety. Hamit Guga, certain that the local authorities would see and hear no evil, was in no hurry to return to his native Kurveleshi. But he had reckoned without the influence of Christaki Zographos. Zographos got a writ, posted a reward and threatened to use his influence in high places to have the local gendarmerie officers exiled to some forlorn outpost unless something was done. With visions of Yemen's scorching sun burning into their skulls, the gendarmerie commander and his men suddenly became quite active. Not long afterwards, Hamit Guga was shot to death.

50.

Bëri Prilli butësirë,
o, Hamit Gugë levendi,
me radhë e zure bastinë
në Dhelvinaq e Vishaninë.

T'was during a gentle April,
Oh Swashbuckler Hamit Guga,
You seized for plunder in a row
Delvinaki and Vissane.[94]

Parë zgjodhe Lunxhërinë,
Qestorati breg e brinjë.
Në kishë e vure borinë;
dyzet gra me barrë shtynë!

First you chose Liountzi,[95]
The hill and ridge of Kestorati.
At the church you sounded the trumpet;
Twenty pregnant women aborted!

N'udhë poqe çiliminë,
o, Hamit, e pyete tynë:
"Ku e ka Kaçua shtëpinë?"
"Të porta me llamarinë."

On the road you found a child,
Oh Hamit, and you asked it:
"Where does Katcho have her home?"
"By the zinc-plated door."

U ngre Hamiti dhe vate.
"Hape, moj, portën hape!
Hape, moj Kaço Janaqe!"

Up rose Hamit and went.
"Open up, hey, open the door!
Hey, open up, Katcho Giannakes!"

Ne divan të Koto Duda,
hidhet valle Hamit Guga.
O, glikoja kupa-kupa
e kish bërë Kaço shkurta!

In Koto Duda's sitting room,
Hamit Guga throws a dance.
Oh, the sweet jam, cup by cup,
Petite Katcho brought to them!

Moj Kaço, moj kuçilere,
kërceve nga një penxhere;
shtatë shpirt se ç'i rrëmbeve.
Edhe Tasen që harove,
në për ta u hodh' e morre!

Hey, Katcho, cunning woman,
You jumped out from a window;
Seven souls in all you seized.
And Tassos whom you forgot,
Back in you went and seized from them!

[94] Delvinaki and Vissane, two of the largest villages of the Pogone region, are presently in free Epirus near the border. The villages of Pogone, some of which are in Greece, extend north to Polytsani and are entirely Greek-speaking. In raids during the period 1868-1874, Hamit Guga and Haxhi Gomara sacked the village of Gouveri, killed three women, seized 120,000 piastres and the altar vessels of the church at Delvinaki. In 1870, they seized another 120,000 piastres from the brothers Psieudes in Vissane. In 1871, they sacked the village of Teriachi and looted the home of Demetrios Thanos in Dolon, carrying off his son, Basil for ransom. The ransom was paid, but Basil was murdered. See Spyros Stoupes, *Pogonesiaca and Vessaniotica, (2 vols.), Corfu 1964, Vol. II, p. 67.

[95] Liountzi is the collective name for eleven villages with a total population in 1908 of 2,980 Christians, 435 Moslems.

51.

Në Sopot u pre derveni,	Your way was cut off at Sopoti,
o, Hamit Gugë levendi!	Oh Swashbuckler Hamit Guga!
Bën dava Hristaq Efendi.	A judgment made Christaki Effendi.
Hristaq Efendi dërgoj:	Christaki Effendi declared:
"Do zini Hamin, a ç'thoj?	"Will you catch Hamit, what say you?
Se mua fjala më shkoj!	For my word is obeyed!
Po s'e zut Haminë,	If you do not capture Hamit,
prapa u dërgoj syrgjynë!"	I'll have you sent on to exile!"
Kur e dëgjoj Xhaviti,	When Xhavit heard it,
treqind lira dha Xhaviti	Thirty pounds gave Xhavit
më u vra deli Hamiti.	To have heedless Hamit killed.

Ottoman despotism and inertia and Albanian terror—Epirus' historic scourges—failed to stay its Christian population's thirst for progress and freedom. Regardless of what language they spoke, the Epirotes created schools and maintained churches in which they learned and used Greek. And through this medium, they maintained contact with the political and intellectual currents of the nineteenth century.

Semi-orientalized, brutalized by an unchanged life in which brigandage and militarism held sway, the illiterate Moslem shepherds and brigands led by feudal lords took little part in this evolution. Generally speaking, this was the situation a century ago and thus it remained at the outbreak of the Balkan Wars. In fact, while the "independent" Albanian state that came after that period made little progress, it did succeed in depriving the Albanophone Greeks of their "window on the world," their schools.

In the 1870's, the irrepressible Christian unrest in "European Turkey" was renewed. In 1875, it was an uprising of the Christian Serb peasants in Bosnia and Herzegovina. A year later, it was Bulgaria, where 60 villages were devastated and 12,000 were massacred as an object lesson to the other *rayas.* The whole of Europe stared at the Constantinople dispatches of *London Daily News* correspondent Sir Edwin Pears in shocked disbelief, and William Ewart Gladstone was moved to write his famous pamphlet on *The Bulgarian Horrors and the Question in the East* in which the Liberal statesman demanded: "Let the Turks now carry away their abuses in the only possible manner, namely, by carrying off themselves. Their zapties and their mudirs, their bimbashis and their yuzbashis, their kaimakams and their pashas, one and all, bag and baggage, shall, I hope, clear out of the province they have desolated and profaned."

To forestall the inevitable reaction of Tsarist Russia to the massacres of Balkan Slavs and Europe's demand for reforms, Turkey's new sovereign, Abdul Hamid II, proclaimed a constitution. Then, when Europe's

diplomats went home from their conference at Constantinople, called
to demand Ottoman reforms, Hamid had the constitution revoked. His
grand vizier, the Smyrnian Midhat Pasha, was exiled to Syria where he
was strangled on imperial orders and his stuffed head sent to the sultan
in a box labeled "Japanese Ivories."

But where diplomacy had not availed, cannons now prevailed and,
on April 24, 1877, Russia declared war on Turkey. The Greek guerrillas
of Thessaly and Epirus once more resumed their operations and Crete
rose up to demand union with the motherland—the only form of self-
determination Greek populations beyond the borders of the Greek state
have ever desired in modern times. The Albanian Moslems needed no
great wisdom to sense that all was not well. An anecdote of those days
told of a rally of Holy War fanatics in Epirus in which one turbaned
sheikh succeeded in whipping up a frenzy. "We will march to Crete
to aid our brothers against the infidels," the sheikh shouted. The roar
of approval had not subsided when one voice in the crowd was heard to
ask: "How shall we march to Crete? It's an island!"

Another tells of a gathering of Labs who were told by a leader that,
"by Allah! We will not give up Crete to the Greeks!" "But, by Allah,
if they take it," he was asked. "Well then," he replied, shrugging his
shoulders, "by Allah, we'll just have to give it!" The circumstances of
the uprising of 1878 and the raid on Lykoursi have been related in a
previous work.[96] Here we shall give the Moslem version in which those
who aided the invaders were held as traitors to the oath they had been
required to swear upholding the Porte.

52.

Shtatëdhjet e tetë seneja,	In Eighteen Hundred and Seventy Eight,
ç'u ndez topi e batareja.	Cannon and gunshot were set ablaze.
Në Likurs u ngre simeja	At Lykoursi the flag was raised
e i folë Turqisë: "Eja!"	And Turkey was bidden: "Come on!"
U çkul Turkija si reja.	The Turks rose up like a cloud.
Ranë poshtë nga xhadeja.	They fell back of the highway.
Dbivrat, paçin lanenë,	The Divrians, damnation take them,[97]
Anagnostërit u ngrenë,	The Anagnostares arose,
Ziso Stavrua me Gumenë	Zeso Stavros with the abbot
trazuan vilaenë.	Betrayed the province.
Van'e qeshën hyqymenë;	They went and fooled the government;
shkeln' kryqin bënë benë.	They trod upon the oath of the cross they
Rrethuan Karalibenë.	had sworn.

[96] See *AC*, pp. 54-55.

[97] Divri, entirely Christian. Pop. (1908), 1,012.

Zunë Fejzo Muhamenë.	They encircled Karali Bey.[98]
I nxuar festen, vun' kapellë.	They seized Fejzo Mehmet.
"Të bësh kryqin tri herë!"	They removed his fez, set a hat on him.
	"Make the sign of the cross three times!"

In after times, it was said, Fejzo Mehmet Abazi did not care to recall publicly the humiliation he had suffered at the hands of the Delviniote insurgents led by Zesos Stavros and the Abbot Philemon of the Theologus Monastery. But the feudarch's descendents, however, apparently remembered. Nearly a century later, his grandson, Sabri, the son of Haxhi Abazi, headed a band of Albanian irregulars who joined Mussolini's invading army in taking Konitsa. Sabri's band pillaged the Greek town, shooting down unarmed civilians. Falling into the hands of the Greeks later, he was tried as a war criminal and shot. But on that day in 1878, when the Greeks of Delvino seized their feudal lord—master of 15 Christian villages—and mocked him in their fashion, they were taking revenge for centuries of abusive serfdom. And, if their action cannot be condoned, it can be understood.

The Albanians were inured to Ottoman defeats by now, but what occurred in Bulgaria, the threshhold of the Turkish capital itself, proved even to the most backward that Turkey in Europe was doomed. The Ottomans under Osman Pasha held out with 50,000 men for nearly five months against the Russians at Plevna, but, on Jan. 9, 1878, they were forced to surrender and the Russian steamroller hurtled on to Constantinople. Adrianople fell on Jan. 28 and an armistice was reached by January 31. But it was not the fervent passion of the Balkan peoples and the anachronism that was the Ottoman Empire that the Albanians blamed for their sultan's plight. That would have been something that was beyond the grasp of the average Moslem tribesman of Albania's highlands. For them, such a defeat could only be due to the treachery of commanders who would not fight, of provisioners who failed to provide. They had been failed, but they were yet to identify the failure with its actual cause. In short, they cursed the manner in which the empire was being run, but it never occurred to them, as it had to every other people in the Balkan peninsula, to curse the empire itself.

This is their view of the defeat in Bulgaria:

53.

Osman Pasha në Pleme të Vogël,	Osman Pasha in Lesser Plava,[99]
Osman Pasha qet dy topa.	Osman Pasha had two cannon.
Qet Moskovi gjashtqind topa.	The Muscovite had six hundred cannon.
Në Pleme të Vogël dridhet toka.	At Lesser Plava the earth trembles.

[98] Karali Bey, Christian. Pop. (1908), 85.

[99] i.e. Plevna.

Dridhet toka tue luftue;	The earth trembles at the fighting;
pashallarët krejt jan' dorëzue.	The pashas utterly gave in.
Osman Pasha ô tue luftue.	Osman Pasha was battling.
Osman Pasha kqyr prej detit,	Osman Pasha came up from the sea,
a s'po i vjen imdat prej mbretit.	But aid arrived not from the king.
Ç'far imdati qi kan que?	What sort of aid was sent to them?
Në vënd të fishekve, sapun kan que!	In the place of bullets, soap was sent!
Në vënd të bukes i qojn' qymyr!	In place of bread, coal was sent.
S'e pat qare pa u bân' teslim.	Without lament they made surrender.

As a direct result, and still as loyal retainers of the Porte, the Albanians formed the famous "League of Prizren" which modern Albanian historians have seen fit to cite as the "Albanian awakening." The assessment of this movement by informed contemporaries and this author in the previous work is somewhat different. The Albanians, encouraged by agents of the Porte which was too feeble to assist them directly, called for: 1) The evacuation of their sultan's territory by its Christian neighbors and 2) The consolidation of all the territories ruled by Albanian Moslems into a single Ottoman unit better able to defend their own and their sultan's interests.[100] Nowhere did the Albanians ask what the other Balkan peoples demanded—that Abdul the Damned get out and leave them masters in their own house.

The luckless raid of Santi Quaranta and Giasta by 150 Epirote irregulars[101] was put down by Ottoman troops that were landed from the troopship *Mahmoudie*. This incident provided the pretext for the confiscation by Sultan Hamid of the olive groves and fisheries of the Santi Quaranta-Delvino coastal area. These were transferred not to the Turkish state, but directly to the personal holdings of Hamid. For this reason his descendents in later years included these lands in their fruitless litigation to recover Hamid's legacy, which included more choice morsels such as the Mosul oilfields of Iraq.

Santi Quaranta itself was in no position to resist. But it was otherwise with the hornets' nests of Nivitsa Boubari and Keparon.

54.

Që në Pisk' e në Sarandë,	From Piska to Santi Quaranta,
u mbush deti me karavë.	The sea was filled with ships.
Dolli sulltani Sarandë	The sultan came to Santi Quaranta
të bënjë imlaqë fshanë.	To make a fief of the villages.
S'm'u ndodh një djal as një vajzë	Neither a son nor a daughter was found me
të lëftonjë me sulltanë.	To battle with the sultan.

[100] *AC*, pp. 55-57.

[101] *ibid*, pp. 54-55.

Përveç nga Nivica, thanë,	Only from Nivitsa, they say,
duall' dy tre kapetanë.	Two, three captains sallied forth.
Dhe nga Qiparoja janë;	They're from Keparon as well;
luftë zunë me sulltanë.	They commence to battle with the sultan.
Fora e bënë me pallë.	An advance they made with sword.
Van' e u vranë me sulltanë!	They go and are slain by the sultan.

The war, for the Greeks, however, was not a total loss, for the consciences of the Great Powers that gathered in Berlin were troubled. The Greeks had few friends among the diplomats who gathered under Bismarck's presidency to redo the map of European Turkey (and undo the too thorough Russian victory embodied in the Treaty of San Stefano.)[102] As a result, Greece would be given a sop. The Greek lands of most of Thessaly and the Epirote port of Arta were to be freed from Ottoman rule, although much else was to remain as it had been.

Such a settlement satisfied nobody. It encouraged the Greeks under Ottoman rule in the rest of European Turkey to believe that their day of liberation was closer and to push public opinion in Greece nearer to the brink of a war of liberation for which Greece was not at all ready. It also aroused the actual masters of those lands to the reality that their days as overlords of the Greek *rayas* were numbered. Their self-assurance and trust in their sultan badly shaken, they alternately cursed their own leaders' apathy, mumbled their disappointment at Sultan Hamid's inability to resist and inwardly steeled themselves to accept the inevitable advance of the Greeks if it proved truly inevitable.

55.

Janina çerek Stambolli,	Yannina, quarter of Stamboul,
dilni, o, t'u mbuloftë gjolli!	Go forth, may the lake drown you!
Dilni se t'u afërua sinori.	Go forth, for they've approached your border.
Hapni sytë, seç u mori	Open your eyes, for you'll be taken
Jorgo dhënderi Moskovi.	By George the bridegroom of Muscovy.
Jorgo dhënderi Rusisë	George the bridegrom of Russia
kërkon vënd e Shqipërisë.	Seeks Albania's land.
O, Jorgo, more jezit,	Oh George, hey you fink,
ke tre vjet që bën tertip	For three years you've misbehaved
sa u hodhe në Gjirit!	Until you threw yourself on Crete!

At the end of June, 1881, the decision having been made in Berlin and accepted reluctantly in Constantinople, the territories granted to Greece were accordingly gathered into the free kingdom. A characteristic incident occurred in Arta where the Turkish governor asked that the raising of the Greek flag not be accompanied with an appropriate salvo of guns

---

[102] *ibid*, pp. 55-56.

because it might offend the touchy sensibilities of the former Albanian masters of the city!

Knowing the yearnings of their Greek helots only too well, the Albanian beys could not attribute this loss of territory to other than the one Greek Epirote whose word carried so much weight in Stamboul, Christaki Zographos. Both their disappointment at a surrender without a fight and their attribution of the same to Zographos are mirrored in the song below:

56.

Nga Serezi vjen haberi;	From Serezi comes the news;
tri herë qëlloji teli.	Thrice the wires rang up.
E qëlloji Hristaq Efendi:	Christaki Effendi calls up:
"Ju, Turqi, inat mos merni;	"Turkdom, hold you not a grudge;
kështu e pru bënë sferi!"	Thus the globe turns 'round!"
Vate Trikalla e sheheri,	Gone is the city of Trikkala,
Vollua shkel e hambari,	The port and warehouse of Volos,
Dumeqeja vënd asqerit,	Domokos the place of soldiery,
Arta hrisafi sheherit.	Arta the golden city.
Qaj, moj, qaj e zeza Artë,	Cry, oh blackened Arta, cry,
se nuk do kthehesh më prapë	For nevermore will you come back
se e kan' vulosur Shtatë!	Because the Seven thus decided!
Ky Sulltan Hamiti, ç'bënë?	What is Sultan Hamid doing?
Qysh të patëm mbret pa mënd	How have we such a careless king
si dhe gjithë këtë vënd	That you would give up all this land
pa ia bërë dyfek 'bëmb?'	Without a rifle going 'bang?'

But there were some—not many—among the Moslems of Epirus who saw that what was being sown by their intransigence was a heritage of hatred that would benefit neither themselves nor their descendents. If, for many of them, Italian encouragement to resist the Greek surge was a welcome hand from an unexpected quarter, for others it was an uneasy portent of evil things to come.

Those who could discern the true shape of things could recall that their fathers in 1847 and their grandfathers in 1828, after spilling their blood to suppress the Greeks, had come to a similar conclusion. Had their wisdom prevailed, their grandchildren and great grandchildren today would not be enduring the misery and terror reigning in the People's Republic of Albania.

57.

Në Stamboll telit i ranë	In Stamboul the wire runs
Janinë përmbi pashanë:	To Yannina unto the pasha:
"Prete Jorgo Kapetanë!	"Await George the captain!
Vulatë s'ia kan' marrë,	Unfixed are the seals as yet,[103]

---

[103] The reference is to the yet unsigned Treaty of Berlin.

kërkon Vlorën e Beranë!	He seeks Valona and Berati!
Frëngjit derit se ç'na dhanë,	The Frankish pigs have turned us over
na bën skllave ndë Junanë!"	To make us slaves of the Greeks!"
Kush të bëjm', bir, ja'llahën?	What are we to do, by Allah?
Pse të mos duam Junanë?	Why should we not want the Greeks?
Ç'do t'a bëjmë Italjanë?	What can we do with the Italians?
Ata na ndrojn' të mbanë.	They will change our ways.
Shok, pse jemi të marrë?	Comrade, why are we possessed?
Kështu se ç'na ke shkruar,	Thus, as it was written for us,
t'a ujdisim me Junanë!	Let us compact with the Greeks!
A mos na prisi imanë?	Would they uproot our customs?
Si e kemi, ato t'a mbamë!	As we have them, so we'll keep them!

Greece had avoided an official confrontation with Turkey in 1878 because she was unprepared. She was not so fortunate when, still unprepared, she was pushed by popular pressure into the disaster of 1897. Although Epirus and the still-Ottoman portion of Thessaly continued to draw their share of the Greek public's heated attention in the period between the Treaty of Berlin and the war of 1897, two issues, one old and one new, claimed the spotlight. The old matter was the as yet unresolved status of Crete where unceasing revolts proclaimed that island's demand for union with Greece. The second was Macedonia, where Greek and Serbian aspirations clashed with those of Bulgaria.

The Bulgarian annexation of Eastern Roumelia on Sept. 6, 1885, resulted in the suppression and expulsion of a long-established Greek minority, giving Greece a foretaste of what would happen should Bulgar designs on Macedonia succeed. Immediately, however, the Bulgarians collided not with Greece, but with Serbia. A Serbian army was annihilated at Svilnica before peace was restored.

Greek Premier Theodore Deligiannes was under great pressure to go to war, and border clashes with the Ottoman forces became more frequent. The Greek army was partially mobilized, but a blockade by the Great Powers forced the government to order demobilization on April 14, 1886. Nevertheless, the bloody events in Crete and elsewhere had mobilized Greek public opinion behind the National Society in its demand that the government respond with positive action to the plight of the people of the still-enslaved parts of Greece.

At the same time, the Society was raising funds and gathering recruits for the insurgents in the Ottoman-occupied territories where the situation threatened to boil over.[104] In 1897, it did, and Greece, unprepared as ever and without allies, rushed headlong into war. Greece's defeat was a foregone conclusion by cooler heads, and, had there not been Great Power mediation in which Russia played an important role, even the

[104] *AC*, pp. 58, 59.

modest gains of 1881 would have been cancelled. The Epirotes, who had enthusiastically expected much from a Greek victory, were grateful that Greece had been able to salvage most of her previous gains from defeat.

58.

Ç'kanë fushat që rrekojnë
nga karrocat që shkojnë?
Top'e xhephane ngarkojnë;
Veleshtino e çkarkojnë.
Me Etem Pashan lëftojnë,
Etem Pasha mjekrëzinë.

What have the plains that they groan
From the carriages that come?
Cannon they bring and ammunition;
They unload at Velestino.
They are to battle with Edhem Pasha,
Edhem Pasha black of beard.

Smolenski ia hipi kalit;
bëri përpjetë malit.
Përpjetë malit në brinjë,
në syt mbante dylbinë.

Smolenski jumped upon his horse,
He took to the slope of a hill.
On the slope of the hill at the edge,
To his eyes he raised his binoculars.

Vështon fush'e Thesalinë
të dy bashk me Kostandinë,
nga do shkoj Etem ordhinë.
E prinë në Veleshtinë
e i vran' kavallarinë.

He gazed on the plain of Thessaly
Together with Constantine
Where Edhem's horde would pass.
They awaited him at Velestino
And they killed his cavalry.

Bëri jurush për n'Athinë,
po u kthe prap' për Janinë.
Çerhdi një teli i ri
përmbi Zotin Kostandi:

He made an advance toward Athens,
But he turned back to Yannina.
A new telegram arrived
For the Lord Constantine:

"Jo dyfek, po dashuri!
Etemi të kthehet përsëri!"

"Not a rifle, but friendship!
Edhem is to withdraw forthwith!"

Etem u fut në Janinë.
Keshmë simaho Rusinë;
na dha gjithë Thesalinë.

Edhem hid himself in Yannina.
We had Russia for an ally;
She gave us all of Thessaly.

Once Greece had digested the lesson of 1897, steps were taken to regain ground. Western European military advisers were imported to do for Greece what Prussian officers were doing for Turkey. Greek statesmen moved closer toward Balkan cooperation so that a future contest would not find the Greek David alone with the Turkish Goliath. Above all, those in responsible positions had to steel themselves against any renewed popular pressure for a premature showdown.

But the unresolved issues of Crete and Macedonia continued to build up steam. In the former case, a safety valve was provided in the creation of the Cretan autonomous state under Prince George of Greece. The Cretans, like the Cypriotes today, recognized the interim nature of their state and, when external obstacles could be overcome, eventually succeeded in their determination to be joined to Greece. Macedonia, however, was a greater problem because it was a stumbling block before a chief pre-condition of any ouster of the Ottoman Empire from its European possessions—an understanding between the Christian states of the Balkans. The crux of the problem lay in the ethnic potpourri of Macedonia where Slavs predominated in the north while, in the regions now part of Greece, the Greek element was numerically superior.[105] The quickly drawn and soon demolished Treaty of San Stefano had allotted the whole of this territory to Bulgaria and neither Sofia nor Macedonia's Bulgarian element had forgotten it. Putting forth a claim far in excess of their ethnic limits, the Bulgarians claimed the whole of Macedonia including the port of Salonica.

Arrogating unto itself the sole right to regard itself as "Macedonian," the Bulgarian element was encouraged to claim the entire three vilayets of Monastir, Salonica and Uskub. It is from this untenable claim that was created, following World War II, the pseudostate of Macedonia under Yugoslav aegis.

Applying this understanding of its slogan "Macedonia for the Macedonians," the Internal Macedonian Revolutionary Organization (IMRO) came into being. The priests and schoolmasters of Greek villages were singled out as special targets for assassination. Its aim was to force the Greek villagers by terror to renounce their allegiance to the Oecumenical Patriarchate and accept both affiliation with the Bulgarian Exarchate and Bulgarian schoolmasters.

Since such a project took considerably more funds than Bulgaria could expend, the IMRO Central Committee ordered large-scale extortion and robbery of the Greeks in the more affluent urban centers of Macedonia. The Albanians, except insofar as it might present a serious threat to the empire's integrity, were gleeful witnesses of the spectacle of Christian murdering Christian in territories where Albanian and Turk were synonymous. With the Albanian-speaking Epirote Greeks, however, the issue was a burning one. Men who had defended their own against the Ottoman enemy were just as eager to defend their brothers against a Bulgarian one. Besides, with Korytsa as an intermediate region of Epirus and Macedonia, they were particularly concerned that a state hostile to Greece might occupy their back door.

Athens, still frightened by the near disaster of '97, would act only when ready—and that might be too late. Something had to be done. By way of the National Society, the leader of a Macedonian Greek guerrilla band, Evangelos Strebeniotes, issued a desperate plea for an experienced

---

[105] As a result of massive exchanges of population with Bulgaria and Turkey, no minorities of any consequence now exist in Greek Macedonia. Greek statistics of 1940 listed a population of 1,491,976 Greeks and 80,345 Slavs, the latter further diminished following the end of World War II. For the story of the exchanges, see Stephen P. Ladas, *The Exchange of Minorities — Bulgaria, Greece and Turkey,* Cambridge, Mass. 1932.

military leader capable of organizing resistance to the Bulgarians. The National Society and sympathetic government leaders agreed this must be done, but a condition was laid down for any volunteers. Nothing was to be done to bring the existence of Greek irregular units to the Turks' attention so as to involve official Greece. To do so would place the Greek state itself in jeopardy.

Private volunteers who would give heart to the Greek villagers and retaliate for any Bulgaromacedonian assaults were sought and found. The man who agreed to lead them was the scion of a distinguished Epirote family—Paul Melas. The son of George Melas and nephew of Leon Melas, the author of the klephtic romance "Gerostathes," Melas was born in 1870 and admitted to Evelpides, Greece's West Point, in 1886. In 1892, he married Stephan Dragoumes' daughter, Natalia. With every reason to reject this impossible assignment, Melas took the command and traveled northward using the pseudonym Mikes Zezas, an Albanian play on his surname (Zeza-Melas: the Dark One).

He crossed the border of Thessaly into Macedonia after buying needed provisions in Larissa on Aug. 23, 1904, sending a message to Germanos Karavangeles, the Metropolitan of Kastoria, informing him of his arrival. A reply from the metropolitan, welcoming him to the soil of Alexander the Great, reached Melas in the village of Kostoratsi. From there, taking every precaution in accordance with his instructions to remain unknown to the Turkish authorities, Melas passed on to other villages—Strebena, Prokopani, Belkameni, Nereti, Negovani. Everywhere he was hailed as a savior by the Greek villagers whom he hoped to organize into an underground militia to resist the IMRO "komitadjis."

It was drizzling continually on October 13 when Melas decided to rest overnight in Siatista before proceeding along the muddy paths to the next point in his itinerary, the village of Korestia. He had no sooner found accommodations for himself and his little band when word was received that a body of Turkish troops would pass through shortly. Melas ordered his men indoors, armed and alert against discovery. The Turks entered and left but, just as suddenly, veered back. Someone had betrayed the strangers' presence.

The Turkish soldiers laid siege to the houses where Melas and his men were quartered and they were forced—despite their orders—to fire back, killing two Turkish soldiers. Melas was called to surrender, but he continued to resist until felled by two shots. A few of his men succeeded afterwards in escaping alive. Some time later, Metropolitan Germanos had his body disinterred at night and reburied with the rites of the Church.[106] All of Greece joined his widow in mourning for Melas, the first national martyr of the Macedonian struggle. He was 34—the same age as Marcos Botsaris when the brave Souliote fell at Karpenisi.[107]

59.

Kush e di, kush e kish parë	Who knows him, who has beheld
Kapetan Pavllo Mellanë?	Captain Paul Melas?
Në Maqedhoni e vranë	In Macedon was slain
Kapetan Pavllo Mellanë.	Captain Paul Melas.
Nga Çatishta me të dale,	From the exit of Siatista,
dy martinë mbas i dhanë.	Two Martini shots from behind they gave.
I thien supin e kranë.	They broke his shoulder and his back.
Zunë kambanat e ranë;	The bells begin to ring;
zonjës van' ia thanë:	To his wife they go and say:
E vranë, zonjë, e vranë	They slew him, madam, they slew
Kapetan Pavllo Mellanë!	Captain Paul Melas!

In death, however, Paul Melas accomplished what he had been unable to do in life. Men of the pen and the sword in both free Greece and the Turkish-occupied provinces turned their gaze toward the hitherto silent drama taking place in Macedonia. The famous and the obscure alike came forward to take part in the struggle.

Of the central committee in Athens whose task was to aid recruitment and arming of the bands we find Epirote names such as Tzavellas and Dangles along with others made bright in other local struggles. Among the officers in the field who succeeded Melas we find a scion of the Chimarriote clan of Spyromelios alongside a direct descendent of Kolokotronis.[108]

Cretan volunteers, fresh from their own fight for freedom and union, alongside men from Chimarra and Argyrocastron, Premeti and Korytsa, enlisted in the ranks of the irregulars assisting the hardpressed Greeks

---

[106] The brave metropolitan was afterwards named a member of the Synod in Constantinople and elevated to the see of Amaseia, but he was later condemned to death by the Turks and fled to Vienna where he died. His remains were brought to Greece and buried with honors in 1959.

[107] Folksongs in Greek mourning Melas' death will be found in Tziatzios, op. cit., p. 8, and Petropoulos, op. cit., p. 173. Greek poets also published many elegies for the brave captain. Among them, better known for his satire, was George Soures for which see *Complete Works, (2 vols.), Vol II, p. 63, Athens, 1954.

[108] Partial lists of the volunteers, indicating rank but, unfortunately, not their birthplaces, will be found in Paul Gypares, *The Pioneers of the Macedonian Struggle, 1903-1909; pp. 312-335, Athens 1962.

of Macedonia. And if today the Greek flag flies over Kastoria, Kozani
and Siatista and even Salonica itself, it is through the sacrifices of such
men inspired by the protomartyr Melas that it does so. Many, in their
eagerness to serve, bought their own weapons in Athens and went off
to the hills of Macedon. The pride with which their kin and countrymen
regarded them is reflected in this song from the region of Argyrocastron.
The subject, leader of a band largely composed of men from his own
district, took leave just long enough to wed before he returned to the
fray, and it was doubtless at his own wedding that the song was first
heard:

60.

Sevo vetu në kurorë	Savvas goes to don a crown
faq e kuqe, mustaq e hollë,	Ruddy of face, with fine moustache,
dyfek Malihjer në dorë.	A Mannlicher rifle in his hand.
Dyfek me shtatë të shtira	A rifle with seven rounds
prurë Sevua në Athina;	Procured Savvas in Athens;
bler-o njëzet e dy lira.	He bought it for twenty-two pounds.

In the districts of Northern Epirus, these lads, many of them no more
than schoolboys, were beheld with especial admiration as the future liberators of their own as well. And indeed, many won their baptism of fire
in Macedonia to be incorporated later in the regular Greek army, return
to their birthplace as liberators and stay—as irregulars once more—to
secure for their native soil the self-rule Europe denied it in handing it
over to the Albanian state.

But, before the irregulars in Macedonia were ordered out and dis-
banded—many to become part of the regular army—the slogans of the
French Revolution were heard in the streets of Salonica and Constantinople, Moslem and Christian embraced and Hamid fell from his bloodstained throne.

The Young Turk movement, *Ittihat Teraki* or Union and Progress,
was born in Paris of the visionary vaporings of exiles and students. It
died in Constantinople in the harsh reality of cynical opportunism. It
was born of a not quite real hope of brotherhood in which all Ottoman
subjects would have a share. It concluded with the 1916 massacres of
the Armenians and Assyrians that could have served as a crude prototype
of Hitler's "solution" of the "Jewish Question." It left as its legacy
Kemal Atatürk's most sinister slogan—"Turkey for the Turks."

It is not our purpose here to trace the movement's progressive de-
generation, but the strong light it casts on the course of events in the
southern Balkans must be accounted. Emerging from the talking stage
in Paris to an active conspiracy in the Second and Third Army Corps in
Salonica, the Young Turk movement made its bid for power on July 23,

1908. Turks and Greeks, Bulgars and Serbs, Armenians and Sephardic Jews all rejoiced in the false dawn. In Constantinople, the fine Albanian nostrils of Hamid's First Army Corps bodyguards smelled out the direction of the wind and, predictably, went with it. Hamid had no choice but to proclaim a constitution and, staging a mock display of compliance, opened parliament in person on Dec. 10.

Typical of many such scenes elsewhere is the characteristic episode in Argyrocastron related by Mammopoulos:[109]

> In 1908, the Greek consul in Argyrocastron with local Greeks desired to receive a Greek delegation come to render congratulations to the *mutesarif* of the town on the occasion of the Turkish constitution. The local Turks[110] threatened massacre. Myfit Bey Libohova suffered much to convince them that the thing was very natural. And when the latter, who was Europeanized[111], kissed the hand of one of the ladies of the delegation, the astounded Turks of the town said *ky ësht kahur!* (He's an infidel!)

A counterrevolutionary stroke by Hamid on April 13, 1909, in which the sultan's agents stirred up a Gheg uprising and attempted to bribe the Albanian guard back to his side, failed. Hamid was sent into guarded seclusion in Salonica and Mehmet Recat, an idiot stupified by years of alcoholic addiction and gilded imprisonment, was trotted out of confinement and girded by his new Young Turk keepers with the sword of Osman. An amnesty was proclaimed. The Greeks dissolved their bands in Macedonia and the Bulgarian "Komitadji" leader Yane Sandansky was feted by the Turks in Salonica. Newspapers circulated freely. But all this proved a mere show in the test of time. And the Albanian disposition toward banditry was hardly softened at all by the show of Ottoman constitutionalism.

Typical of conditions in Epirus in this period is this incident culled from letters sent on July 11 and 14, 1909 to the Patriarchate of Constantinople by Metropolitan Neophytus of Paramythia. The Thesprotian prelate relates how, on July 6, fifteen Greek villagers of Plesevitsa were on their way to Phyliates when they were waylaid by bandits led by Muharem Reshet of Kotsika. A woman was fatally shot and one youth died later of wounds. The village priest, George Simas, was wounded in the encounter and fell into the bandits' hands. Father George, a poor man who left three young children, was spitted and roasted alive in the tradition of Tsaoush Prifti and Athanasius Diakos.

[109] *Epirus*, Vol. I, p. 39.

[110] Read Moslems.

[111] His wife was Italian and Myfit Bey himself had a Greek education.

But the time soon drew nigh for Greece, Serbia and Bulgaria to present a joint demand that broken promises of truly equal rights for non-Moslems and provincial reforms be honored. The ultimatum was presented on October 15, 1912, the same day Turkey signed a treaty with Italy virtually ceding Tripolitania to the latter. Montenegro had gone to war a week earlier, beginning a siege of the town of Shkodra which was not to end for many months. "If the Porte desires to accept these proposals," the Balkan states told the Young Turk generals, "order and tranquillity will be reinstated in the provinces of the Empire, and a desirable peace will be assured between Turkey and the Balkan States, which have hitherto suffered from the arbitrary and provocative measures adopted by the Porte toward them."

For the Christian states of the Balkans, the war which began on October 18 was the culmination of the hopes of millions of serfs for five centuries. For the Albanians, it was something else. Ismail Qemal Vlorë, interviewed in Trieste, told the *Wien Frei Presse* correspondent, as reported on August 27, 1912, "None should expect secession of the Albanian movement. The Albanians feel themselves to be Ottomans and their only desire is to collaborate in the renewal and progress of Turkey."

On September 16, in a dispatch from its Constantinople correspondent, Berlin's *Vossische Zeitung* quoted another of Albania's "founding fathers," Dervish Hima, who, being interviewed, categorically stated, "The Albanian movement never had either independence or secession from Turkey as its purpose. Whoever maintains such is a libeller. The conduct of the Turkish Army in Albania was exemplary."

And, while the Greek Army began its operations in Epirus and the day of liberation drew nearer for the Christians, another Albanian notable, Hasan Basra Bey of Dibra, was reported in the *Tribuna* of Rome on October 8 expressing the conviction, "As in 1897, thus this time as well, the Albanians cannot forget that they are Moslems and will defend the endangered integrity of the Turkish Empire against the quadruple alliance. . . . Albania will not seek her independence, but will remain loyal to the empire. She is therefore determined to undertake her defense against the incursion of her enemies."

THE STOLEN VICTORY
(1912-1916)

The Greeks believed they were going to war to free their enslaved brothers. At last, an end would be brought to the unfinished task laid upon them as the legacy of the warriors of 1821.

The Albanians went to war—summoned for the last time by their sultan—to defend their place as the Ottoman presence in the still-occupied Balkan provinces. Part of this "defense"—as always—consisted of a reign of terror by the more or less irregular Albanian Moslem "redifs" in the Christian villages of Epirus. The Labs and Çams sharpened their axes and knives, cleaned their guns and readied the woven goathair sacks they would put to use to carry off plunder. Good use was found for all these implements.

Sacked and put to the torch before the Greek Army's arrival were the villages of Choika, Glyky and Potamia in the vicinity of Preveza; Kamouzades, Skamneli, Tsepelovo, Phrangiades, Liaskovetsi, Phlampouri-ari and Vovousa in the Zagori of Yannina; Alpochori, Manoliasa, Keramitsa and Phortopia in Thesprotia; Limpovon, Plesevitsa, Chlomos, Arachova, Kokkino Lithari, Reveni, Alikos and Parakalamos in Pogoni. Most dramatic was the fate of Nivitsa Boubari, St. Basil, Ondessovo, Loukovo and Pikerni in the district of Delvino. No strangers to resistance, the villagers knew by heart the tale of their destruction and flight to Corfu in Ali Pasha's day.

Touched off by an ill-advised attempt by Greeks to create a diversion by landing at Santi Quaranta nearby[112], this holocaust was reenacted fully in December 1912. Italian correspondent Luciano Magrini of *Il Secolo* told his readers how "the Albanian bands, after the Greeks retreated, fell like wild hordes upon the Greek villages, murdering, looting and setting them ablaze.

> The inhabitants, abandoning their villages and seized with panic, fled to find salvation, walking for many hours in the craggy Acroceraunian hills until they reached the inhospitable cape's sandy shore where they hoped Greek ships would come and save them.

[112] *AC*, pp. 64, 65.

How many of the aged, how many children and how many women were unable to endure the cold of that terrible and fearsome night? How many lost their way? How many who were unable to flee were slain? The records do not say.

High flames rose up from the hills throwing their tragic glare toward the sea so that one might have thought that volcanoes had erupted. The villages of Pikerni, Loukovo, St. Basil and Nivitsa were burning, set ablaze by the Albanian bands.

The wind blew strongly, bearing off the sparks toward the Adriatic sea where innumerable flames shone, both large and small. And the refugees, awaiting the arrival of the Greek craft, warmed themselves from the glow of those flames to escape the shivering cold.[113]

And as they were being evacuated to Corfu, the ragged inhabitants of Nivitsa mourned:

61.

Nivica në rrez' të malit,	Nivitsa at the mountain's root,
të qëllon topi sulltanit	The sultan's cannon smites you
se ti je kalaja e Junanit.	Because you are Greece's fortress.
Nivica është pun' e madhe;	A great labor is Nivitsa;
treqint mijë grosh livadhe.	Three hundred thousand piastres.
Nihna, o, Kakomej e Madhe![114]	Aid us, oh Great Kokamia!

There was another fire, however, that warmed the hearts of the sorely-tried Epirotes—that the hope of liberation was becoming a reality with each passing day. St. Cosmas the Aetolian, "Equal of the Apostles,"[115] had foretold in the days of Kurd Pasha that the *raya* would be liberated in the year when Annunciation Day and Easter came together. In 1912, they coincided and, wherever the liberators went, they were greeted with the double salutation: "Christos Aneste! Hellas Aneste!"[116]

With the fall of the stronghold of Bizani, the surrender of Yannina was a foregone conclusion. Essad Pasha of Yannina (not to be confused with Essad Pasha Toptani of Shkodra), had no choice but to hand over the city on March 6. On hand to accept his surrender were Crown Prince Constantine and General (then colonel) Panagiotes Dangles, a native of

---

[113] Luciano Magrini, *Le Isole, L'Albania e L'Epiro, Maggio 1912-Giugno 1913: stampa delle corrispondenze inviate al "Secolo,"* Milano, p. 262.

[114] Nivitsa's monastery of Kokamia possessed a Gospel manuscript reputed locally to be by the hand of the Apostle Luke himself and to have miraculous properties. After many adventures since the Balkan wars, it is now in safekeeping in Athens. Someday, perhaps, the word of Christ may again be read from it in the village that guarded it for so many centuries.

[115] See *AC,* pp. 35, 36.

[116] "Christ hath arisen! Greece has risen!"

Premeti and later a member of Venizelos' World War I revolutionary triumvirate in Salonica.

62.

Janinë, e zeza Janinë,	Yannina, blackened Yannina,
pa dil e sheh seç asqer vijnë,	Sally and see the army coming,
rreth kalas dyzet mijë!	Forty thousand around the fort!
Kostandini me Dangllinë	Constantine and Dangles
Esat Pashën e thirrë:	Called out to Essad Pasha:
"Do të falesh me të mirë?"	"Will you submit in goodly wise?"
Esat Pasha, kur digjoj,	Essad Pasha, when he heard,
vuri fjalë dhe qëndroj.	Weighed the words and pondered.
Qyçet i dorëzoj;	He surrendered them the keys;
kokën duaj të shpëtoj.	He wished to save his head.

With Yannina's liberation, the advance of the Greek Army into the province of Argyrocastron became little more than a triumphal procession. Little resistance from the beaten Turko-Albanians was encountered as each historic town and hamlet beheld a dream of centuries turn into an intoxicating reality. Everywhere Epirote Christians spoke Albanian, their song was:

63.

Bajraku me kryq e lule	The flag with cross and flowers
tunde, Kostandini, tunde!	Waves, oh Constantine, it waves!
Në Janinë që lëshove,	Where you let it loose in Yannina,
tunde, Kostandini, tunde!	It waves, Constantine, it waves!
Gjirokastër që gëzove,	Where you made Argyrocastron glad,
tunde, Kostandini, tunde	It waves, Constantine, it waves,
bajraku me kryq e lule!	The flag with cross and flowers!

Their homes destroyed and their possessions pillaged, the refugees on Corfu made their way back, still fearful lest the Albanians return, but eager to resume their lives beneath the protection of their own flag. A French journalist, setting forth from Corfu to witness and report what was happening, wrote:

> Night had now fallen. The chimes from a neighboring church tower had just announced eleven o'clock. In St. George Square, the restaurant keepers were taking in the chairs. From a distant piano came the strains of the duet from *Tosca*. Corfu, island of delight, settled herself for sleep, while across there, on the far side of the channel, the peasants of Nivitza, Lukovo and Pikerni were encamped, trembling and apprehensive, in the ruins of their dwellings which the Albanians had burnt.[117]

[117] René Puaux, *The Sorrows of Epirus*, Chicago 1963, pp. 22, 23.

Now these victims of the Albanians also lifted their heads and called upon their former masters and foes to bow before the harbingers of a new day:

64.

Dita duke gdhir' e Martë,	On the dawn of Tuesday,
mblidhuni, o, agallarë.	Gather ye, oh, aghas.
Delni në Mulli të Bardhë;	Go forth to the White Mill;
delni të shihni Junanë	Go forth to see the Greeks,
të pritni Jorgon e parë	To await George the First
që ka pjell e bërë djalë:	Who fathered a son born to him:
Kostandinin me pallë,	Constantine with a sword,
ay që morri Bezhanë!	He who took Bizani!

Gone was Ali Pasha's curse. Gone were the days filled with humiliation and the nights filled with terror. Where for five centuries had stood the blood-red standard of the Crescent now flew the azure colors of the Cross. Typical of celebrations in each of the Christian villages in the former sanjaks of Argyrocastron and Korytsa was the one that took place on May 21, 1913—St. Constantine's Day—in the village of Erinti. Long had the village square, to the inhabitants' shame, been known as the Square of Mohammed. Now, the villagers sang exultantly, it would be known as Constantine's.

65.

Vate maj njëzet e një,	On the Twenty First of March,
ditë e Kostandinitë,	On Constantine's feast day,
ajasmo në lëm u bë;	A blessing was held on the square;
Muhameti mos thoni më,	Do not call it Mohammed's more,
Lëmi i Kostandinitë!	T'is the Square of Constantine!
Humbi vulën Muhameti;	Mohammed has lost his seal;
u bë Kostandini mbreti!	Constantine has become king!
Na kish marë zëmra datë;	Our hearts were filled with terror;
kusarët nat' për natë	The robbers night after night
na mbredhë në për shtëpi.	Went round about our homes.
S'na lan lopë dhe dhi!	They left us neither cow nor goat!
Na i marrnë nga ara,	They took them from our fields,
i vënë kope përpara.	They drove them herd before them.
Të na rroj mbret i ri!	Long may our new king reign!
Pam një dit' eleftheri!	We have seen a day of freedom!
Shkojmë udhën pa mbodhi,	Without hindrance we walk the road,
pa frik; s'na nget njeri.	Without fear; no man disturbs us.

The Epirotes had won their freedom and, with the coming of their own, were assured of their rights to the eternal verities of civilization— life, liberty and the pursuit of happiness. But the death sentence on these rights was passed neither in Argyrocastron, Korytsa, Yannina nor Athens. It was formulated in Vienna—where another death sentence, on the whole of Europe, would soon be uttered. It was concurred in by Rome, where the absolute mastery of the Adriatic Mussolini would attempt to achieve was already a blueprint. And it was in London, on May 30, 1913, that the machinery for carrying out the sentence was created.[118]

Already, the Turkish defeat had left the Albanians masterless. The pasha of Shkodra eyed the whole country. The brother of Grand Vizier Ferid Pasha was ready to declare Albania a sovereign state at Valona. It remained for the gentlemen of Vienna and Rome to make certain the vacuum of power was filled by creatures of their own choosing, and they evolved a plan how this was to be done. Serbia was given half of Albania inland—the present "Kosmet" in Yugoslavia—as a consolation for waiving demands for a port on the Adriatic. The Greek government in Athens, unsupported by its former Balkan allies, could only bow to the pressure to evacuate the northern districts of Epirus to a "protected" Albanian state to serve as the hinterland to the Albanian port of Valona.

To give the crime legal sanction, a commission was ordered to go through the motions of determining Albania's southern (but, note well, not northeastern) boundaries on the ground of language alone. This would insure that, no matter how much the victims might cry out they were Greeks, they could be told solemnly that, after all, they must be Albanians because Albanian was their mother tongue.

What would happen when Greece withdrew and the improvised forces of Albania's Prussian monarch, Prince Wilhelm von Wied, would take over? What would these bandits, still clad in remnants of their Turkish uniform, do to their helpless victims? Schools, churches, homes and lives hung in balance, but it was only spheres of interest that engaged the mapmakers of Vienna and Rome. Thus, on December 25, 1913, Northern Epirus was included in Albania by fiat of the Ambassadorial Conference in Florence. Europe's decision was made without considering the desires of the 130,000 men, women and children involved, and could only be annoyed that these Balkan peasants presumed to the right of determining their own destiny, for this was what the Northern Epirotes did.

Politicians, military, clergy, merchants and peasants—to a man—were determined to interpose their rights between the Great Powers' demands and Athens' reluctant acquiescence. A Panepirotic Assembly in Argyrocastron spelled out the only alternatives its people would accept. Barring the continuation of Greek sovereignty over them, they would accept the nominal rule of Albania as a federalized and, internally, entirely autonomous state.

George Christaki Zographos was made the assembly's spokesman in giving a reply to the note ordering the Greek administration to pull out

[118] *AC*, pp. 69-83.

of Argyrocastron and Korytsa. The formal reply, given to each of the representatives of the Great Powers on February 9, 1914, was couched in the language of Europe's chanceries. The popular reply was more defiant:

66.

Çjanë këto që na thonë?	What is this they tell us?
Frëngu mbreti na dërgojnë!	A Frankish king they send us!
Neve Vidhinë s'e njohmë	We will not accept Wied
se kemi vografon t'onë!	For we have our Zographos!

Zographos' note itself deserves to be given here in its entirety:[119]

The Panepirotic Assembly gathered in Argyrocastron has charged us to request that you agree to call the attention of your Government to the conditions created for the Greek Orthodox Christians who have been put in Albania's possession by the declaration of the Powers.

The populace of Epirus truly believed it had the right to hope that Europe, tearing it away from Greece and stripping it of the freedom it has enjoyed for more than a year, would at least think to safeguard its existence and its ethnic heritage it was able to preserve intact through five centuries of harsh tyranny.

It hoped that, rather than dispose of it like a herd, they would give it guarantees it would itself deem effective in applying to its own political constitution, the polities of European States, and particularly Switzerland, presenting many such examples.

Such being the new State's composition in being made up of so many heterogenous elements and without ethnic or religious cohesion, a special organization was required by it to be capable of dispelling each misgiving, of safeguarding property, of mediating the aspirations of the now divided and mutually hostile elements and of allowing them to develop in peace and safety.

But the Power's Note is silent on this subject.

Nevertheless, we believe it is impossible for Europe to be ignorant of the fate that awaits the Greek populace it wishes to hand over to Albania—a populace whose number, according even to Ottoman statistics, is greater than 130,000 and which comprises the majority in the areas sacrificed.

With regard to ourselves, who have been subject for so long to their excesses, it is not possible to nurture chimaerical hopes. Neither the empty promises, the presence of certain foreign organizers at the head of armed Moslem bands, nor the good will of the Prince, could grant us the least guarantee. At most, a guarantee of this sort could be found only in international occupation sufficient to assure our existence and our national liberties. Otherwise, we are certain that our presently so peaceful and prosperous land will be turned over to the worst anarchy.

Under these conditions and in the absence of a solution that would suffice to safeguard Epirus, a solution it would have been otherwise so easy to discover, the Epirote populace is forced to declare to the Powers

[119] Reprinted in G. A. Drinos, *"Liberty or Death;" Chronicles of the Northern Epirote Struggle, 1914.* Athens, 1966, pp. 100, 101.

that it cannot submit to their decision. It will declare its independence and will struggle for its existence, its traditions and its rights.

But, before it executes this last decision, Epirus turns for the last time to face its judges and pleads with them to modify their decision by which a whole people is condemned.

This people hopes that the Powers will be pleased to make known to it, the sole interested party, their final decision.

May Christian and civilized Europe, by this decision, escape the heavy responsibility for the horror of a ruthless struggle.

Zographos

The plea fell on deaf ears. In appealing to Europe's conscience, Zographos had, perhaps, touched the most insensitive spot of all. Once Austria had delivered the revolutionary Rhegas to his Turkish executioners, and the men at the Ballplatz had wept no tears. Once an English governor had sold a territory under his protection to an Albanian murderer, and no British foreign secretary lost a night's sleep on that account. And no European power was exactly guiltless in courting the bloodstained degenerates who sat on Stamboul's throne while the heads of those who preferred freedom adorned the palace gates.

But, perhaps, there was some good faith in Europe's act if we grant it was born of abysmal ignorance. The European statesmen's homes had never been looted by the Albanians. *Their* kin had never been murdered, raped nor sold into slavery by them. More than the geographic configuration of a Balkan backwash and how it related to their other interests, the statesmen of Europe really did not care to know.

How completely Athens had, at this point, surrendered to the overwhelming pressure was demonstrated in clashes between units of the Greek regular army and armed Epirote villagers attempting to force a stay of execution of their death sentence. While the Greek administrators tried to accomplish their obligation to hand rule to Albania, Epirote soldiers and officers deserted and were declared outlaws. Zographos himself, Demetrios Doulis, a native of Nivitsa who undertook the task of organizing the armed locals, Spyromelios who led the Chimarriotes, and hundreds of others were among those thus condemned. The exultant Albanians, freed of the unpalatable prospect of equality with the *raya* openly taunted the Christians:

67.

Kostandino i mjer,	Oh wretched Constantine,
erdhe për një copë her'.	For a short time you came.
Ikën me robën të çjerr.	In tattered clothes you go.
Na le morat në der'.	You leave us lice on the doorstep.
T'erdhi vahti për rembull,	Your time for seizure has arrived,
o, moj Dropulli me vull!	Oh thou Dropolis renowned!

And the Christians replied in kind:

68.

O, ju të zezë Shqipëtare,   Oh, ye blackened Albanians,
Djalli çuka për të marre   May the devil come and take you,
që në plaku ngjer në djali!   Old and young alike!

Greece nevertheless evacuated the territories and the drama sped to its inevitable end—the proclamation of the Autonomous Republic of Northern Epirus. This was its Declaration of Independence:

Epirotes:

Gathered in Argyrocastron, the Constituent Assembly of delegates summoned by the will of the people has declared the formation of the Autonomous State of Northern Epirus, comprising the provinces the Greek Army is forced to abandon.

In accordance with the Constituent Assembly's decision, the permanent regime of the Autonomous State formed will constitute a new Constituent Assembly to convene when circumstances allow. Temporarily, however, all the powers in the Autonomous State will be exercised by a provisional Government mandated to govern and administer the land in accordance with the fundamentals of equality and justice, freedom of conscience and protection of the lives, honor and property of citizens irrespective of their religion.

Epirotes:

The Constituent Assembly gathered in Argyrocastron has carried out these decisions realizing that our country is in peril, condemned by the powerful. One after another, our aspirations were ignored. They have torn us from the embrace of Greece, our mother. They deny us independence. They deny us self-government within the Albanian State. They even deny us such guarantees as would guard the security of life, of religion, of property and of our ethnic existence. They have brought us to complete despair. Neither the presence of certain foreign officers at the head of unruly mobs, nor the well-meaning intentions of the prince, nor pompous oration, nor the temporary presence of the Greek Army make Epirus safe.

Our ancestral land today lies prey because of the unjust and invalid will of all of the earth's mighty. But our right, the right of the Epirote People to determine its own fate, to organize politically and militarily to guard its independence, remains undaunted. Because of this inalienable right of each people, the Great Powers' desire to create for Albania a valid and respected title of dominion over our land and to subjugate us is powerless before the fundamentals of divine and human justice. Neither does Greece have the right to continue in occupation of our territory merely to betray it against our will to a foreign tyrant.

Free of all ties, unable to live united under these conditions with Albania, Northern Epirus proclaims its independence and calls upon its citizens to undergo every sacrifice to defend the integrity of the territory and its liberties from any attack whatsoever.

Argyrocastron,   The Provisional Government
 Feb. 15, 1914   George Ch. Zographos, president
          Basil of Dryinoupolis
          Germanos of Korytsa
          Spyridon of Vellas and Konitsa, members.

The formation of the autonomous government was the prelude to a struggle brought to an end on May 17, 1914 with the signing of the Protocol of Corfu by the Northern Epirote leaders and the International Control Commission. By this instrument, the victorious Epirotes' demand for self-rule was recognized.[120] Still nominally subject to the Albanian principality, Northern Epirus attained an internationally recognized status that its citizens believed would lead, in time, to reunion with Greece. Thus they saluted the protocol's signing:

69.

Shtatëmbëdhjet të këtija,	On the present Seventeenth,
na erdhi aftonomija;	Autonomy came to us.
Zografi në kryesija	Zographos as the leader
na pruri eleftherija.	Has brought us freedom.
Zografi biri Kristaqit,	Zographos the son of Christakis,
djali yn' të Qestoratit,	Our child from Kestorati,
Dhulli e Kristaq të tjerë	Doulis and Christakis both
na prunë frymë të erë!	Have brought us liberty's breath!

The Northern Epirotes had snatched back their stolen victory. Despite skirmishes on their borders, they believed themselves safe. They could not foresee in May that little more than a month later the Europe that had bowed to their stubborn courage would be no more. The pistol shot rang out in Sarajevo and World War I began.

Meanwhile, the fragile experiment in Albanian independence ended in failure. The former pasha of Shkodra, having been made Wied's minister of war, ousted the prince and plunged Albania into anarchy. Some Albanians cast their fortunes with Austria-Hungary and Germany. Others looked to Italy while still others longed nostalgically for their vanished sultan to raise above them once more the Star and Crescent. This anomaly, of course, was in itself a voiding of the Corfu Protocol since there was no longer a *de facto* Albanian principality to which Northern Epirus must remain attached. The reunion of Northern Epirus with Greece in October was seen by the Northern Epirotes as a veritable Second Coming. They assured themselves that Korytsa, Argyrocastron and the rockbound coast of Chimarra would now be one with the rest of Greece forevermore.

What had actually occurred they would realize only later. Italy had occupied Valona as Albania's "protector" and Italy's allies declared they would voice no protest if Greece occupied Northern Epirus *on the same grounds*. Only later, after the seating of Northern Epirus' freely elected deputies in the Greek Parliament, did they realize what this meant: that Greece had been allowed back only to pacify the territory and keep it, as it were, in storage to hand to a restored Albanian state.

---

[120] Complete text in *AC*, pp. 91-93.

Greece resisted this interpretation until internal strife—the proclamation of a pro-Allied government under ousted Premier Eleutherius Venizelos in Salonica against the neutralist royal government in Athens, forced the issue. The blood that had been spilt for five centuries, the struggles of 1912 and 1914 had all been in vain for the Northern Epirotes. Now, under the "protection" of the shield of Savoy, all the horrors they had feared would be heaped upon them. They would have to wait for twenty four years before catching another glimpse of freedom and then return to martyrdom.

EPILOGUE
(1916- ?)

The Italian occupation of Argyrocastron, with France for a time in Korytsa, ushered in the attempt to erase a people's past by the very root. This attempt has not ended. The bulk of the Christian population was deprived of its self-sustained Greek schools and oft-times semi-literate Albanian teachers usurped the classrooms, the metropolitans of Dryinoupolis (Argyrocastron) and Korytsa were exiled to Greece and Albanian was ordered substituted as quickly as possible in the Churches.

To be sure, the occupiers and their successors found Christian collaborators, few though these were. Some such had espoused Albanian nationality abroad as a result of heavily subsidized propaganda. Some betrayed for pay and position. Others gave in out of despair. In the Greek-speaking villages, instruction in Greek was resumed partially after 1921 as a result of a codicil signed by Albania in joining the League of Nations. Then it was whittled away gradually by successive Albanian governments until the Grecophone minority had successful recourse in 1934 to the Hague Tribunal.

Today, the Communist regime permits primary education in some Greek-speaking border villages where children are taught the ABCs of atheism, Bolshevism and worship of Enver Hoxha in a barbarous "people's" Greek. A newspaper—the *People's Tribune*—is even published for them in that peculiar idiom in Argyrocastron so that they may better understand their master's will. But the Albanian-speaking Greeks, severed from their brethren linguistically, are officially Orthodox Christian Albanians—nothing more. No Albanian regime has seen fit to allow the least recognition of their actual desires and no Albanian regime ever will. Their position, despite the few to whom a secondary role under Moslem tutelage was assigned, was that of a suspected minority in a preponderantly Moslem state. This position is accurately portrayed by the Moslem editor of the newspaper *Demokracija* of Argyrocastron in 1931. Wrote Xhevat Kallajxhiu, who was later to serve as Argyrocastron's mayor by Nazi appointment in 1943:

109

Two Moslem Albanians terminate their discussion on the appearance
of a Christian and two Albanian Christians end their talk upon the
approach of a Moslem. Why should we hide it? If the Turkish borders
were near we would be Turks in conscience, just as the Christians look
to Greece.[121]

Such ties could not be severed by brainwashing in the schools, by
blustering propaganda in every form and by all the pressures (including
naked terror) that the state had—and has—at its command. They could
only be driven underground and never professed publicly or within ear-
shot of a Moslem.

They developed an elliptical way of expression which was not unknown
during the worst years of Ottoman rule. Thus, when the authorities
secretly set a Lab brigand, Idriz Jaho, to slay a village priest on May 28,
1931, the following lament by the villagers hints at the reason for the
crime:

70.[122]

Në Nokovë ç'bë një thamë?	What wonder was wrought in Nokovon?
Në Shën Eli në të dalë,	At Saint Elias at the exit,
mu të porta në të hirë,	By the entrance door,
na vranë priftin e mirë.	They killed our good priest.
O, Papadhimitri ynë,	Oh, our Father Dimitris,
pse të vranë nuk e dimë.	Why they killed you we know not.
Na çuditë Lunxherinë.	T'is a wonder to us in Liountzi.
Qanë djemtë në Athinë.	Your children weep in Athens.
Vraja jote shum' e madhe,	Your terrible murder
u mësua në shtatë krale:	Was learned in seven kingdoms:
në Servi, në Vullgari,	In Serbia, in Bulgaria
në të zezënë Greqi.	And in blackened Greece.
Mingulli dhe Nokovë bashk	Mingouli and Nokovon together
të vunë ulerimë.	Let them give lament.
Të përmblodhën pleqësinë,	Let the elders be gathered,
se ato qi u bën tarshtinë	For what has now occurred
s'jan'bërë dhe me Turqinë.	Had not happened even under Turkey.

Who "they" are is never spelled out, but the mention of the priest's
children in Athens and the recollection that what had occurred "had not
happened even under Turkey" tells all. The priest was evidently too out-
spoken a "Grecomane" and was therefore silenced. His murderer went
unpunished.

<hr/>

[121] Cited by Mammopoulos in *The Myth of Albanian Collaboration in the Independence of Greece, address delivered May 13, 1963 before the Epirotic Society of
Athens. Pub. by the Society, Athens 1963.

[122] See also AC, p. 130.

The end of the regime of King Zog and the formal annexation of the Albanian crown by Italy could hardly improve matters. A year later, Mussolini declared war on Greece. As a result, Northern Epirus was freed briefly by the Greek army before Hitler stepped in to save his sad sack ally. The following song contains no "Aesopian language" but is straight to the point, composed as it was at the height of the unexpected and superb Greek victory. It recalls not only Greece's victories on land, but the Greek contribution to the Allied victory at sea as well.

71.[128]

Vjen një telegram urxhent	An urgent telegram is sent
në Athin' në Qifisha.	To Athens, to Kephisia.
E dërgon Duçja vet:	It is sent by the Duce himself:
"Lësho vëndin, Metaksa!"	"Give up the country, Metaxas!"
"Së lëshoj, merre vet,	"I won't surrender, take it yourself,
pse Greku ashtu e ka.	For that's how it is with the Greek.
I kam ormisur çolenjtë	I shall hurl the Evzones
me fustanella të ra.	With their brand-new kilts.
Të dërgosh Alpinistenjtë	Send for the Alphinists
të lëftojnë me ta."	To do battle with them."
Në Kalpaq bëjnë të pjek,	They make contact at Kalpaki,
tek ura në Kalama.	By the bridge of Calamas.
S'bëjn' dyfek, po bajonet;	They used no rifle, but bayonet;
Mben gjysmët mbi ta.	Of them half survived.
Treqint papor vërviti.	Three hundred ships were hurled.
Nga treqint mben dhe ea.	Some of the three hundred survived.
Të treqint, të gjith' i mbyti;	The three hundred were sunk;
rrofte "Papanikolla"!	Long live "Papanikoles!"

Twenty four years of the "Republic" and "Kingdom" of Albania, five centuries of the Ottoman Empire, all had failed to destroy the soul of this people. Albanian spokesmen abroad told the world again and again that it did not exist until some of them began to believe their own lies. A few months of reunion with Greece, although under the most precarious conditions, had proven otherwise.

Men in Albanian uniform deserted the ranks into which they had been impressed to turn their guns on their tormenters. The majority of the "Christian Albanians" turned out to greet—and assist—the Greek army in Argyrocastron, Premeti, Korytsa and wherever the Flag of the Cross advanced. The bishops of Korytsa and Argyrocastron, both natives of Korytsa whose Albanian credentials had hitherto been unchallenged, came out to bless the Greek troops and to urge them on to victory.

But what of the other side? The Albanians had raised scarcely a

[128] *AC*, pp. 146-153.

finger to save their king. They had pledged their unwavering loyalty to Mussolini and his Axis partner and, in return were granted the spoils—Kossovo and Paramythia (Çamërija). But there was one account that they had to settle with the "Christian Albanians," with the Northern Epirotes who spoke Albanian and thought Greek. The Axis occupation of the whole of Greece gave them the chance. To detail the bloody sequence of events that transpired under Italian occupation to 1943 and under Nazi occupation until late 1944 is to recall a story told and documented in *Albania's Captives*.[124] Suffice it is to say that scarcely a Christian village in Northern Epirus escaped arson, pillage and massacre.

The forces contending on the soil of Northern Epirus were a shifting mosaic in miniature of the total Balkan picture—with complications. There were the Northern Epirotes themselves, initially operating as units of General Napoleon Zervas' republican but anti-Communist EDES. There was, later to be sure, the trojan horse of the Communist-organized Greek EAM working in tandem with the Tito-inspired FNÇ of Enver Hoxha. And there were on the other side, besides the foreign occupation, the Albanian Fascist militia and the anti-guerrilla "chetas" of the Balli Kombëtar or Nationalist Front.

The same guarded language noted earlier is used in the following lament. It gives itself away to those who sing it by comparing, with mournful pride, the destroyed villages' beauty with that of Greece's proudest ancient monument.

72.

Moj e shkreta Lunxhëri,
jeshe bukura stoli.
Të kishin gjithë zili;
u dogje, u bërë hi.

Oh you barren Liountzi,
A beautiful ornament were you.
All were jealous of you;
You were burned, they made you ash.

Të vunë zjarrë anëmbanë
Italija me Gjermanë.
Vetëm Dhoksatin e lanë
se kish karshi kasabanë.

They set you ablaze from top to bottom,
Italy with the Germans.
Only Doxati the left
Because it was across from the market.

Kush e dogji Lunxhërinë,
më e bukurë krahinë
si Akropol në Athinë,
gjith' arhond e zotërinjë?

Who was it who burned Liountzi,
The most beautiful place
Like the Acropolis in Athens,
All pride and nobility?

It was not difficult for the Albanian nationalists whose sway now extended into Greece's portion of Epirus as well to persuade the Germans or their predecessors that Greek guerrillas were being hidden near the Christian villages. However much they would deny it, it was not difficult, either, for the Italians and Germans to know how unloved their ilk was in Epirus and other parts of occupied Greece.

[124] pp. 154-172.

On the other hand, until their might waned, the Axis administrators knew they could count on their Albanian friends. How did the obscene act of revenge commence? The following ballad obtained by the author from Northern Epirote refugees in Greece after the war directly confirms a rich store of documentary evidence:

73.

Mu n'teqe së Gjirokastrës	In the *teke* of Argyrocastron
shum' bejllerë mbjedhur janë	Many beys gather together
edhe në kuvëndin thanë:	And in consultation say:
"Shkojm' të digjemi Krishtjanë	"Let us go and burn the Christians
se mbi 'ta kemi inanë."	Because we've a feud with them."
"Myslimane me Gjermane	"The Moslems with the Germans
do të prishëm Grekomane	We'll destroy the Grecomanes
që na janë din-dushmane,	Who are enemies of our faith,
se të mos rrëmbejm' shtëpinë	For if we do not sieze the house
s'bën për neve Shqipërinë!	Albania shall not be for us!
Me ata ne kemi gjak;	With them we have a feud of blood;
erdhi dit' të marrëm hak!"	The day has come to take revenge!"
Në komandatura vanë	To the headquarters go they
edhe komandanti thanë	And to the commander say
që me syt të vetë panë	That with their own eyes they have seen
shum' andart ne malë janë	There are many guerrillas on the hill
dhe ndë fshatra pin' e hanë.	And in the villages drink and eat.
Edhe komandanti tha:	And the commander quoth:
"Merr' ca oficjera, pra,	"Take, then, some officers,
edhe sot ne jemi gati	Even now we are prepared
bashk' të vemi ngjer në fshati.	To go together as far as the village.
Me mitralloz e dinamiti	With mortars and with dynamite
Grekomanetë të vriti!"	Kill the Grecomanes!"
Ashtu bëjnë radh' mbë radhë	Thus wrought they shoulder to shoulder
Adolf me "Shqipëri së Madhë."	Adolf with "Greater Albania."

Abandoned, persecuted, devastated, the Northern Epirotes were the victims of one final betrayal—British and American support of the Communist-controlled Balkan "resistance" organizations of the NOF and EAM in Yugoslavia and Greece and the FNÇ in Albania. Whatever armed resistance the Northern Epirotes themselves were able to scrape together was either absorbed into the FNÇ, scattered and then destroyed or absorbed into the EDES and forced to center its operations further south in a struggle as much against the Communists as against the Axis occupation.

And, after the war when it was too late and the West realized the monsters it had helped create, it was the emigrated remnants of the Albanian collaborators of the Fascists and the Nazis that were regarded by the West as the legitimate opponents of Albanian communism. With

Tito's NOF established as the People's Federative Republic of Yugoslavia, Enver Hoxha's FNÇ filled the power vacuum left by the Ballists
and Germans. Tito's break with Moscow was Hoxha's signal to choose
Stalin over Tito. Moscow's reconciliation with Tito was Albania's cue
to tie up with Mao Tse-tung.

Instead of justice at the Paris peace table, the Northern Epirotes saw
Greece's attempt to rescue them withdrawn and sent to the Council of
Foreign Ministers where it was postponed *sine die*. Hundreds fled into
free Greece to find themselves in the midst of an attempted Communist
takeover foiled only by British and then American support of the legitimate government of Greece.

Behind Enver Hoxha today looms the shadow of Ali Pasha, and behind
the ruling clique in Tirana is the spirit of the Lab beys and aghas of yore
who foreswore their nation and faith for the blandishments of position,
power and privilege. Much has changed, but this has remained. The
çifçi of yore is the *"koperativist"* of today and toils in a serfdom more
abject than any for his master, the state. And the state is a clan of
familially interrelated party careerists who maintain the Stalinist system
in all its terrifying absurdity.[125]

Of course, the secular religion of Marxism-Leninism in its Stalinist
manifestation is the "established church" of the country and Islam is
played down, although it would be too much to say, as one observer
does,[126] that it is "in its death throes." The Albanian Orthodox Church,
none of whose nominal bishops in Albania are canonical and all of whom,
in fact, are agents of the "Sigurimi," the Red Gestapo, is in the process
of liquidation.

In the villages of Northern Epirus, a few aged priests are allowed to
do no more than offer an occasional divine liturgy. Marriage is secular-
ized, baptism rare and burial without clergy is common. And when these
few priests die, they are not replaced, the churches henceforth standing
locked "because the people no longer have need or desire for them."

Even in the towns and in Albania's capital itself, the process of de-
stroying them goes on relentlessly. One example suffices. St. Procopius,
on the edge of Tirana, was one of the city's two Orthodox churches
in pre-World War II days. Since then, the city has grown, and with it
the number of Orthodox from the south who find rural life impossible

---

[125] Radio Moscow, on Feb. 10, 1962, noted that "half or more of the 53 members
of the Central Committee of the Albanian Party of Labor are related" and proceeded
to unravel the geneology thereof. Despite subsequent shuffles, the latest being in
September 1966, this "clan" continues to retain the key posts in its hands. See
William E. Griffith, *Albania and the Sino-Soviet Rift*, Cambridge, Mass. 1963, pp.
320, 321.

[126] Harry Hamm, *Albania—China's Beachhead in Europe*, New York, 1963, p. 55.

and are not allowed to emigrate. The church, according to the observer cited above, "has been converted into a restaurant. The altar has been turned into a counter, on which a chromium-plated coffee machine is displayed as the latest 'socialist achievement.' " Where the ikons once stood are batteries of bottles of cheap Albanian liquor. The nave is full of tables, at which the new class consumes its *kelab* and *shashlik* to the wailing sounds of popular songs."[127]

But there are other songs that the Northern Epirotes carry in their hearts and which are heard on the other side of the grim Greco-Albanian frontier. They speak of loyalty to the faith the Red tyrants are striving to uproot and of a centuries-old struggle to live free as Christians and as Greeks. They speak of heroes and martyrs who pitted themselves against tyranny. And they enshrine a forlorn hope that may yet bloom again. America's Walt Whitman spoke for all such as them when he wrote:

> When liberty goes out of a place, it is not the first to go,
>   nor the second or third to go,
> It waits for all the rest to go—it is the last.
> When there are no more memories of martyrs and heroes,
> And when all life, and all the souls of men and women are
>   discharged from any part of the earth,
> Then only shall liberty, or the idea of liberty, be dis-
>   charged from that part of the earth,
> And the infidel come into full possession.[128]

[127] *Ibid.*, p. 54.

[128] *To a Foil'd European Revolutionnaire.*

APPENDIX A

(from p. 22, n. 30)

He had not ended the speech, what followed he had not said,
When, behold, the Turks fleeing, both on foot and horesback.
Some fled while others said: "Damned may you be, my pasha.
A great ill brought you to us this summer.
So many Turks have you destroyed, both spahis and Albanians."
And Botsaris gave shout with the sword in hand:
"Come, pasha! Why do you take it badly and flee in haste?
Turn back here to our land, to Kiapha the barren,
Here to set up your throne, to become even a sultan!"

Τρία πουλάκια κάθονταν στοῦ Ἄϊ Λιᾶ τὴ ράχη
Τ'όνα τηράει τὰ Γιάννενα, τἄλλο τὸ Κακοσοῦλι·
Τὸ τρίτο τὸ καλύτερο μοιρολογάει καὶ λέγει·
-Μαζώχτηκ' ἡ ἀρβανιτιὰ πάνω στὸ Κακοσοῦλι
Μὲ τρία μπαϊράκια πέρασαν τὰ τρία ἀράδ' ἀράδα,
Τ'όνα'ταν τοῦ Μουχτὰρ Πασσᾶ, τ' ἄλλο τοῦ Μέτσο Μπόνου
Τὸ τρίτο τ' ὀμορφότερο, ἦταν τοῦ ξυλυφτάρι.
Μιὰ παπαδιὰ ἐφώναξε ἀπό ψηλὴ ραχούλα·
-Ποῦστε παιδιὰ τοῦ Μπότσαρη, παιδιὰ τοῦ Κουτσονίκα;
Οἱ Τοῦρκοι μᾶς πλακώσανε, θέλουν νὰ μᾶς σκλαβώσουν.
στὸ Τεπελένι νὰ μᾶς πᾶν τὴν πίστι μας ν' ἀλλάξουν.
κι' ὁ Κουτσονίκας χούγιαξε ἀπό τὸν Ἀβαρίκο·
-Νὰ μὴ φοβάσαι, παπαδιὰ, μὴ σοῦ περνάει στὴ γνώμη.
Τώρα νὰ δῆς τὸν πόλεμο, τὰ κλέφτικα ντουφέκια
Πῶς πολεμᾶ ἡ κλεφτουριὰ κι' αὐτοὶ Κακοσουλιῶτες.

The above text in Albanian ends at this point. The Greek text continues:

Τὸν λόγον δὲν ἀπόσωσε, τὴν συντυχιὰν δὲν εἶπε,
Νὰ ἰδῆς τοὺς Τούρκους κι' ἔφευγαν πεζούρα καὶ καβάλλα,
'Αλλ' ἔφευγαν κι' ἄλλ' ἔλεγαν "Πασσᾶ μ' ἀνάθεμά σε.
Μέγα κακό μας ἔφερες τοῦτο τὸ καλοκαίρι
'Εχάλασες τόση Τουρκιά, σπαῆδες κι' ἀρβανῖτες."
Κι' ὁ Μπότσαρης ἐφώναξε μὲ τὸ σπαθὶ στὸ χέρι·
-Ἔλα, πασσᾶ! Τί κάκιωσες καὶ φεύγεις μὲ μεντζίλι;
Γύρνα ἐδῶ στὸν τόπο μας, στὴν ἔρημη τὴν Κιάφα,
'Εδῶ νὰ στήσης τὸ θρονί. νὰ γένης καὶ σουλτᾶνος !

APPENDIX B

(from p. 47, n. 56)

At midnight, in his guarded tent,
    The Turk was dreaming of the hour
When Greece, her knee in suppliance bent,
    Should tremble at his power:
In dreams, through camp and court, he bore
The trophies of a conqueror;
    In dreams his song of triumph heard;
Then wore his monarch's signet ring:
Then pressed that monarch's throne—a king;
As wild his thought, and gay of wing,
    As Eden's garden bird.

At midnight, in the forest shades,
    Bozzaris ranged his Suliote band,
True as the steel of their tried blades,
    Heroes in heart and hand.

There had the Persian's thousands stood,
There had the glad earth drunk their blood
    On old Plataea's day;
And now there breathed that haunted air
The sons of sires who conquered there,
    With arm to strike and soul to dare,
    As quick, as far as they.

An hour passed on—the Turk awoke;
    That bright dream was his last;
He woke—to hear his sentries shriek,
    "To arms! they come! the Greek! the Greek!"
He woke—to die midst flame and smoke,
And shout, and groan, and sabre-stroke,
    And death-shots falling thick and fast
As lightenings from the mountain cloud;
And heard, with voice as trumpet loud,
    Bozzaris cheer his band:

    "Strike—till the last armed foe expires;
    Strike—for your altars and your fires;
    Strike—for the green graves of your sires;
        God—and your native land!"

They fought—like brave men, long and well;
    They piled that ground with Moslem slain,
They conquered—but Bozzaris fell,
    Bleeding at every vein.
His few surviving comrades saw
His smile when rang their proud hurrah,
    And the red field was won;
Then saw in death his eyelids close
Calmly, as to a night's repose,
    Like flowers at set of sun.

Bozzaris! with the storied brave
　　Greece nurtured in her glory's time,
Rest thee—there is no prouder grave
　　Even in her own proud clime.
She wore no funeral-weeds for thee,
　　Nor bade the dark hearse wave its plume
Like torn branch from death's leafless tree
In sorrow's pomp and pageantry,
　　The heartless luxury of the tomb;
But she remembers thee as one
Long loved and for a season gone;
For thee her poet's lyre is wreathed,
Her marble wrought, her music breathed;
For thee she rings the birthday bells;
Of thee her babe's first lisping tells;
For thine her evening prayer is said
At palace-couch and cottage-bed;
Her soldier, closing with the foe,
Gives for thy sake a deadlier blow;
His plighted maiden, when she fears
For him the joy of her young years,
Thinks of thy fate, and checks her tears;

　　And she, the mother of thy boys,
Though in her eye and faded cheek
Is read the grief she will not speak,
　　The memory of her buried joys,
And even she who gave thee birth,
Will, by their pilgrim-circled hearth,
　　Talk of thy doom without a sigh;
For thou are Freedom's now, and Fame's:
One of the few, the immortal names,
　　That were not born to die.

BIBLIOGRAPHY

Abbott, G. F., *Macedonian Folklore*, Cambridge, 1903. (Rp. Chicago 1967).

Albania, *Basic Handbook*, London, 1943-44.

Amadori-Virgilj, Giovanni, *La Questione Rumeliota e la Politica Italiana, Biblioteca Italiana di Politica Estera, No. 1*, Bitonto, 1908.

Amery, Julian, *Sons of the Eagle, a Study in Guerilla Warfare*, London, 1948.

Andreades, A. *La Grèce devant le Congrés de la Paix*, Paris, 1919.

Antonopoulos, Stamatios, **The Treaties of London, Bucharest and Athens*, Athens, 1917.

Apostolakes, Giannes, **The Folksong*, Athens, 1929.

Aravantinos, Panagiotes, **Chronicle of Epirus* (2 Vols.), Athens, 1856.

—————, **Epirus Folksong Collection*, Athens, 1880.

—————, **Biographical Collection of Learned Men during the Turkish Occupation*, Ioannina, 1960.

Aravantinos, Spiros P., **History of Ali Pasha Tepelenli*, Athens, 1895.

Argyrocastrites, Nicholas, **The Sons of the Mercenaries*, Vol. I, Athens, 1956.

Argyropoulos, Pericles J., **Greece's Claims*, Athens, 1945.

Asteriou, Asterios, **The Greco-Slavic Boundaries: Macedonia-Thrace-Albania, with an appendix concerning autonomous Albania*, Athens, 1916.

Athene, Winter, 1963, Vol. XXIII, No. 4, Chicago, Ill.

   1963, Vol. XXIII, No. 4, Chicago, Ill.

Baerlein, Henry, *Under the Acroceraunian Mountains*, London, 1922.

Baud-Bovy, D., *L'Epire, Berceau des Grecs*, Geneva, 1919.

Bekker, Immanuel (ed.), **Historia Politica et Patriarchica Constantinopoleos/ Epirotica*, Bonn, 1869.

Birge, J. K., *The Bektashi Order of Dervishes*, London, 1937.

Callimachos, Demetrios, D.Th., **The Civilization of Northern Epirus*, Ioannina, 1959.

Carapanos, Alexis C., *Memoire sur L'Epire du Nord*, Paris, 1919.

—————, *Appel Adressée à la Conférence de la Paix au nom des Populations de l'Epire du Nord*.

Capps, Edward, *Greece, Albania and Northern Epirus*, Chicago, 1963.

Cassavetes, Nicholas J., (Brown, Carroll Neide, Ph.D., ed.) *The Question of Northern Epirus at the Peace Conference*, N.Y., 1919.

—————, ed., *Greek Northern Epirus, a Peace Conference Issue*, N.Y., 1943.

Cassavetti, Demetrius J., *Hellas and the Balkan Wars*, London, 1914.

Central Committee of Northern Epirotes (KEBA), *Memorandum to the United Nations Special Committee on the Balkans, Sub-Committee III on Refugees and Minorities, Prot. No. 5139, Jan. 26, 1948* (mimeo.).

Charisiades, Stylianos, **Northern Epirus Enslaved*, Athens, 1951.

Chasiotes, G., **Collection of Folksongs for Epirus*, Athens, 1866.

119

Christopoulos, Constantine P., *The Greek Problem, Thessalonica, 1945.
Comstock, John L., M.D., History of the Greek Revolution, N.Y., 1828.
Cordighiano, P. F., La poesia epica di confine dell'Albania del Nord. (Collana studi sui paesi dell Illyricum No. 5). Venezia 1943.
Dimitsas, Mergaritis, *Critical Researches on the Origin and Nationality of George Castriotis, Scanderbeg, Athens, 1877.
Dominian, Leon, Frontiers of Language and Nationality in Europe, N.Y., 1917.
Driault, Edouard, La Question d'Orient, Paris, 1920.
—————, and Lheretier, Michel, Histoire diplomatique de la Grèce, Paris, 1925.
Drinos, G. A., *Freedom or Death: Chronicles of the Northern Epirote Struggle, 1914 (Memoranda, Protests, Referenda, Proclamations, Circulars, Telegrams, Rallies, Articles, Debates in the Greek Parliament, Illustrated), Athens, 1966.
Dropolitans in Athens, Union of, *Dropolis in Northern Epirus, an Almanac, Athens, 1965.
Elliot, Sir Charles, Turkey in Europe, London, 1908.
Epirotiki, Hestia, Jannina 1952.
Eton, William, Survey of the Turkish Empire, London, 1798.
Evangelides, Demetrius E., *"The Antiquities and Byzantine Monuments of Epirus," in Neos Hellenomnemon, (Spyridon Lambros, ed.), Vol. X, Athens, 1913.
—————, *The Ancient Inhabitants of Epirus, Athens, 1947.
—————, *Northern Epirus, Athens, 1919.
Fauriel, Charles, Chants populaires de la Grèce moderne, (2 Vols.), Paris, 1824-25.
Folklorit, Instituti i, Mbledhës të Hershëm të Folklorit Shqiptar, 1635-1912, (3 Vols.), Tirana, 1962.
Gazes, George, *The Triumph of Delvinakion, Aegina, 1835. (2nd ed. Athens, 1916)
Germanus, Julius, The Role of the Turks in Islam, in Islamic Culture (pub.), Vols. VII-VIII, 1933-34.
Giankas, Athanasius Ch., *Epirotic Folksongs, 1000-1958, Athens, 1959.
Gibbons, Herbert Adams, New Map of Europe, London, 1915.
Gibbons, Hugh (ed.) The Ciano Diaries, 1939-1943, Garden City, N.Y., 1946.
Greek Documents, Series B., No. 1, (Military Questions), Report of the Greek Government Concerning the Greek-Bulgarian and Greek-Albanian Frontiers, Submitted to the Secretariat of the Foreign Ministers' Council of the Four Great Powers, Paris, 1946.
Greek Ministry of Foreign Affairs, The Greek White Book, Diplomatic Documents Relating to Italy's Aggression Against Greece, Washington, D.C., 1943.
Greek Under-Secretariat for Press and Information, The Conspiracy Against Greece, Athens, June, 1957.
Gregoire, Henri, *Digenes Akritas, N.Y., 1948.
Griffith, William E., Albania and the Sino-Soviet Rift, Cambridge, Mass., 1963.
Halimi, Kadri, Narodna Poezija Siptara u Selu Lesane u Podrimi, in ZBORNIK RADOVA Etnografski Institut, Srpska Akademija Nauka, Beograd, 1951.
Hamm, Harry, Albania—China's Beachhead in Europe, N.Y., 1962.
Hammer-Purgstall, J. V., Geschichte des Osmanischen Reiches, (10 Vols.), Pest, 1827-35; 2nd ed. (4 Vols.), 1840.
Hasluck, F. W., Christianity and Islam Under the Sultans, 2 vols., Oxford, 1929.
—————, "The Nonconformist Moslems of Albania," Contemporary Review 127 (1925), pp. 599-606.
Haxthausen, Werner, Neugriechische Volkslieder, Munich, 1935.
Helmreich, Ernst Christian, The Diplomacy of the Balkan Wars, 1912-1913, London, 1938.

International Justice, Permanent Court of, (Hague Tribunal), *Fascicule No. 64, Series A./B., XXXIV Session, Minority Schools in Albania, Advisory Opinion of April 6, 1935.*

Istorisë e Gjuha, Instituti i, *Istoria së Shqipërisë,* Tirana, 1959.

Jacomoni di San Savino, Francesco, *La Politica dell'Italia in Albania,* Rome, 1965.

Kantiotes, the Very Rev. Archimandrite Augustine N., **St. Cosmas the Aetolian, 1714-1779* (2nd ed.), Athens, 1959.

Keramopoulos, Antonios D., **The Greeks and their Northern Neighbors,* Athens, 1945.

Kersopoulos, Jean G., *Albanie: ouvrages et articles de revue parus de 1555 à 1934,* Athens, 1934.

Koliqi, E., *Epica Popolare Albanese,* Padova, 1937.

Kolleger, Willibald, *Albaniens Wiedergeburt,* Vienna, 1942.

Kolokotrones, General Theodore, *Memoirs. The Greek War of Independence,* Chicago, 1967.

Kriares, Aristides, **Cretan Songs,* Chania, 1909.

Külçe, Süleyman, *Osmanli Tarihinde Arnautluk,* Izmir, 1944.

Kyritsis, Photius P., *The Question of Northern Epirus,* N.Y., 1946.

Ladas, Stephan, P., *The Exchange of Minorities—Bulgaria, Greece and Turkey,* Cambridge, Mass., 1932.

Lambertz, M., *Die Volkpoesie der Albaner: Ein einführende Studie.* Serajevo, 1917.

Lamprides, John, M.D., **Epirotic Studies: Description of the City of Yannina,* Athens, 1887.

Lebeque, Pierre, *Pyrrhos,* Paris, 1957.

Legrand, Emile, *Bibliographie Albanaise,* Paris, 1912.

—————, *Recueil de chansons populaires Grecques,* Paris, 1873.

Lelekos, Michael, **Folksong Anthology,* Athens, 1852-53.

Lilles, John, **Liountzi: History, Folklore, Manners and Customs,* Athens, 1947.

Maccas, Leon, *La Question Greco-Albanaise,* Paris, 1921.

Magrini, Luciano, *Le Isole, L'Albania e L'Epiro, Maggio 1912-Giugno 1913: Ristampa delle Corrispondenze Inviate al "Secolo," Milano.*

Makrigiannes, General John, **Memoirs,* Athens, 1947.

Mammopoulos, Alexander Ch., **Epirus: Folklore, Customs, Ethnography* (2 Vols.), Athens, 1961-64.

—————, **The Myth of the Albanian Contribution to the Independence of Greece,* Athens, 1963.

—————, **Emigration and the Demotic Song,* Athens, 1964.

Mann, S. E., *Albanian Literature,* London, 1955.

Manouses, A., **Ethnic Songs,* Corfu, 1850.

Marchiano, M., *Canti Popolari Albanesi,* Foggia, 1908.

—————, *Poesie Sacre Albanesi,* Napoli, 1908.

Mariott, Sir John A. R., *The Eastern Question,* Oxford, 1925.

Merlie Melpo, **Songs of Roumelia,* Athens, 1931.

Mertzios, Constantine D., **Mikros Hellenomnemon,* Ioannina, 1960.

Metallinou, Angelica B., **Our National Claims: Northern Epirus,* Thessalonica, 1950.

Michaelides, Costas A., **Parga: Her History from Olden Times to the Present,* Athens, 1960.

Michalopoulos, Phanes, **Gregory the Argyrocastran and the Revolt of Euboia,* Athens, 1955.

—————, **Moschopolis, the Athens of Turkish Times,* 1500-1769, Athens, 1941.

Miller, William, *The Ottoman Empire and its Successors,* Cambridge, England, 1934.
Morison, W. A., Ph.D. (tr.), *Revolt of the Serbs Against the Turks, (1804-1813),* Cambridge, England, 1942.
Mylonas Peter, *Beneath Hoxha's Boot,* Athens, 1959.
Neos Kouvaras (Pub.), 1961- (Annual of Epirote Chronography), Athens.
Nicol, D. M., *The Despotate of Epiros,* Oxford, 1957.
Noli, Fan S., *George Castrioti Scanderbeg* (1405-1468), N.Y., 1947.
Noti Botzaris, D., *Carte des Églises et des Écoles helléniques de l'Epire du Nord en 1913,* Athens, 1920.
—————, *Carte Ethnographique de l'Epire du Nord en 1913,* Athens, 1919.
Oekonomides, A., *Songs of Olympus,* Athens, 1881.
Oikonomides, D. B., *"The Folksongs of Northern Epirus: Part I, Emigration Songs," Dedication to Chr. Soulis,* pp. 37-45, Jannina, 1956.
Papadakis, B. P., *Documents officiels concernant l'Epire du Nord, 1912-1935,* Athens, 1935.
Papadopoulos, N. G., (Katsomitros), *The Popular Muse,* Athens, 1907.
Papadopoulos, Nicholas K., (ed.) *Northern Epirus: Essays by Fifth Form Students at the Tositsaion-Arsakion School,* Athens, 1959.
Papamanolis, Th. G., *Flameswept Epirus: The Awful Drama of the Inhabitants of Thesprotia and the Collaboration of the Albanians with the Axis, 1940-1944,* Athens, 1945.
Paparrhegopoulos, Constantine, *History of the Greek Nation,* Athens, 1930. (3 Vols.)
—————, (Daskalakis, Apostolos, ed.), *Condensed History of the Greek Nation,* Athens, 1955.
Papastavrou, Christos B., *Greece and Northern Epirus,* Athens, 1945.
Passow, A., *Popularia Carmina Graeciae Recentioris,* Leipzig, 1860.
Patselis, Nicholas B., *Northern Epirus and Her Natural Boundaries,* Athens, 1945.
—————, *Delvinakion in Epirus,* Athens, 1948.
Peace Through Justice League, ed., *La Participation de l'Albanie a la Guerre Mondiale, 1939-1945,* Athens, 1946.
Pedersen, H., *Zur albanesischen Volkskunde,* Copenhagen, 1898.
Peristeres, Spyros, *Folksongs of Epirus and the Morea in Byzantine and European*
Pernot, Humbert, *Chansons Populaires Grecques,* Paris, 1931.
      Notation, Athens, 1950.
Perrhaebus, Christopher, (Hadjivasiliou, Chrysaphes), *Greek Revolution, Collected Works,* Athens, 1956.
Petriaew, A., *Albaniya i Albantsii,* in *Russkaya Mysl',* Petrograd, Vol. V., 1915.
Petropoulos, Demetrios, *Greek Folksongs* (2 Vols.), Athens, 1959.
Photos, Dr. Basil J., *The History of Northern Epirus Through Postage Stamps,* Chicago, 1963.
—————, *Epirus and Epirotic Muse,* Chicago, 1963.
Pipinelis, M. P., *Europe and the Albanian Question,* Chicago, 1963.
Polites, Nicholas G., *Selections from the Songs of the Greek People,* (3rd ed.), Athens, 1932.
Pop, Alexander G., *This is Albania,* Athens, 1946.
Pouqueville, Charles François, *Travels in Greece and Turkey,* London, 1820.
Pouqueville, Charles François, *Histoire de la Regeneration de la Grece,* Paris, 1824.
Puaux, René, *The Sorrows of Epirus,* Chicago, 1963.
Rentis, Constantine Th., *The Northern Epirote Question,* Athens, 1922.
Robinson, David M., *America in Greece; A Traditional Policy,* N.Y., 1948.
Ruches, Pyrrhus J., *Albania's Captives,* Chicago, 1965.

Sathas, Constantine N., *Turkish-Occupied Greece, 1453-1821, Athens, 1869.

Selenica, Teqi, Shqipëria me 1927 (Ministry of the Interior, pub.), Tirana, 1928.

Shay, Mary Lucille, The Ottoman Empire from 1720 to 1734 as revealed in Dispatches of the Venetian Baili, Urbana, Ill., 1944.

Sigalos, Louis, The Greek Claims on Northern Epirus, Chicago, 1963.

Skenderes, Constantine, *History of Autonomous Northern Epirus, 1913-1916, Athens, 1930.

Skendi, Stavro, Albania, N.Y., 1956.

————, "The Northern Epirus Question Reconsidered," in Journal of Central European Affairs, Vol. XIV, July, 1954.

————, Albanian and South Slavic Oral Epic Poetry, (Memoirs of the American Folklore Society No. 44), Philadelphia, 1954.

————, "The South Slavic Decasyllable in Albanian Oral Epic Poetry," Slavic World, IX, No. 4., pp. 339-349.

Solomos, Dionysios, *Complete Extant Works, Athens, 1965.

Soures, George, *Complete Works, (2 Vols.), Athens, 1954.

Spyromelios, Miltos M., *Greece and Albania, N. Y. (n.d.)

Stergiopoulos, C. D., *The Northern Boundaries of Epirus, Athens, 1945.

Stockman, Doris und Erich, und Wilfried Fiedler, Albanesische Volksmusik, (East) Berlin, 1965.

Stoupes, Spyros, *Pogonisiaca and Vessaniotica (2 Vols.), Patras, 1962.

————, *The "Foreigners" in Corfu, Corfu, 1960.

Tarsoule, Georgia, *Morean Songs of Corone and Methone, Athens, 1944.

Theros, Agis, (Theodoropoulos, Spyros), *Songs of the Greeks, (2 Vols.), Athens, 1951.

Tommaseo, Nicolo, Canti Popolari Toscani, Corsi, Illirici, Greci, (4 Vols.), Venice, 1841-42.

Toynbee, Arnold, Greek Policy Since 1882, London, 1914.

Trapmann, A. H., The Greeks Triumphant, London, 1916.

Tsopanakos, P., *Warrior Songs of the Struggle for the Independence of Greece, Athens, 1878.

Tziatzios, Evangelos St., *Songs of the Sarakatsans, Athens, 1928.

Tzovas, Costas I., *To Northern Epirus: Laurels and Chains, Athens, 1964.

Venizelos, Eleutherius K., Greece Before the Peace Conference, Paris, 1919.

Vlachogiannes, Giannes, *Klephts of the Morea, 1750-1820, Athens, 1935.

Woodhouse, C. M., The Greek War of Independence; Its Historical Setting, London, 1952.

Zalocostas, George, *Works, (Beneficial Books Society ed.), Athens, n.d.

Zambelios, S., *Folksongs of Greece, Corfu, 1852.

Zotos, Demetrius A., The National Conscience of Northern Epirus through the Centuries, Athens, 1940.

INDEX

INDEX

INDEX